Fear Can't Have Me

Overcoming Fear With The Truth

Live Fearless + Love Fierce!
Sabrina L Klassen

By:
Sabrina L Klassen

Fear Can't Have Me

Overcoming Fear With The Truth

©COPYRIGHT 2019 Sabrina L Klassen

ISBN: 9781086881561

All rights in this book are reserved. No part of this book may be reproduced in any form without prior written permission of the author.

ENDORSEMENTS

Sabrina has written a masterpiece! 'Fear Can't Have Me,' is that book! If you really want fear eradicated once and for all, this book is for you. Sabrina breaks it down step by step to get you from fear into victory. I highly recommend this book to everyone!

Dr. Jeremy Lopez
Identity Network, Inc.
www.indentitynetwork.net

'There is no fear in love; but perfect love casts out fear, because fear involves punishment, and the one who fears is not perfected in love.'
1 John 4:18

Sabrina has written an excellent book dealing with the roots of fear and the process for overcoming. Rooted in her personal experience, she provides practical, biblical insights into living the overcomer's life. I highly recommend her and her work.

Stan E. DeKoven, Ph.D. MFT
Founder and President
Vision International University
www.drstandekoven.com

CONTENTS

Foreword 4

Introduction 5

Section I Fear Lost Love Won

Chapter 1 Not By Choice 10

Chapter 2 The In-Between Seasons 18

Chapter 3 Reality Of The Spiritual Realm 22

Chapter 4 The Year Of God's Grace 27

Chapter 5 The Identity Thief 32

Chapter 6 The Thief Comes To Steal, Kill, And Destroy .. 35

Chapter 7 The Healing Begins Through Obedience 41

Chapter 8 Fear Still Owned Me 46

Chapter 9 The Turn Around 50

Chapter 10 The Release 59

Chapter 11 Re-Defining A Fearless Identity 63

Chapter 12 The Pressing, A Soul Cleanse 66

Chapter 13 Search My Heart, Oh God 75

Chapter 14 Stretching Is Painful 79

Chapter 15 It's His Perfect Love 84

Chapter 16 Fear Can Not Have Me 89

Section II Free From Fear & Rooted In Holiness

A 7-Day Devotional Study On The Letters Of The Apostle Peter

Day 1 – You Are Set Apart 94

Day 2 – Stay Humble 101

Day 3 – Stay Aligned 107

Day 4 – Rejoice In Suffering 113

Day 5 – Like Precious Faith 120

Day 6 – Make Your Choosing Sure 126

Day 7 – Discernment Is Vital 132

FOREWORD

It has been said that people may argue with you about doctrine or the interpretation of Scripture, but they can't argue with your testimony. This is what Sabrina gives you in her book, an unfiltered, raw and transparent testimony of her personal journey to freedom.

You may not agree with every sentiment or theological interpretation, but one thing you can't argue is the truth of who she is today!

As her pastor for the last 8 years, I can personally attest that Sabrina is more free and more fierce than ever thanks to Christ and the freedom that is found in knowing Him. Regardless of your past or present, this same freedom is possible for you as well. You don't have to be perfect or have it all figured out. You just need to be willing, obedient and have a little faith that what God has done for others, like Sabrina, he will do for you.

Here's to your freedom journey!
Scott A. Page
Founding Pastor and Sr. Leader
Liberty Church International
Weatherford, OK

INTRODUCTION

Can I really be fearless? That was the question I asked for many years. Overcoming fear was something I personally never viewed as possible. I remember the days that I would dream of leading worship and teaching the Word of God with a passion that doesn't end. I've had these dreams from childhood. I remember as a very young child using a brush as a microphone and a broom as a guitar, singing and playing my heart out to the music in my head as I led a congregation that didn't exist into worship. At times, my older brother would join and help out with this vision inside of me. He would even pretend to preach the service. I also remember that I would attempt to play every piano I passed by because I absolutely loved music and knew that gift was placed in me by God! I just knew!

But here is where the problem arose. I was absolutely scared to death of being in the public eye. Honestly, I was scared of everything, and it was paralyzing my life. I remember by the age of 27 I had pretty much determined that I would just have to keep dreaming these amazing dreams because reality told me that I would never reach them, or I should say *fear* told me I would never reach them.

Yes, you read that right! Fear was reality to me; I had lived in fear from such a young age that it was all I knew. At 25 years old, the desire for ministry began to rise up in me in a strong way, but the fear continuously reminded me that I was afraid of public speaking, I was afraid of people's thoughts towards me, and I was afraid of failure. The fear of the "what if" was strong.

There came a point about 14 years ago that the gripping, paralyzing fear began to exhaust me. I couldn't fight the call God had placed on my life anymore, but I couldn't do what He asked because I would get sick every single time I even attempted it.

Don't get me wrong here—I was raised in a non-denominational, demon-busting, God-fearing church, and I couldn't count the times I rebuked, went to the altar, or had others pray over me to get set free from this intense fear. You see, fear is a spirit we allow into our lives through many different avenues, such as movies, music, and putting ourselves in fearful life situations, among other outlets, but because fear is a spirit, it can also be allowed into our lives at a very young age due to what others allow us to experience. It can also be connected to a familiar spirit that follows your family line, which is something you can quickly tell if you come from a line of people who are fearful with an ungodly, unnatural fear.

Around the age of 28, I began to learn more about spiritual roots, soul-ties, and temperament. This started me on a journey to my freedom. The first question I asked was, "Where did this fear come from?" This is the journey on which I would like to take you. I am sharing this with you not because I want you to know everything about my life but because I want you to see how the enemy uses the smallest things in our environments to feed on the imperfections in our temperaments, thus creating chaos and destruction in our lives and in our purpose. I want you to see how negative situations can create negative behaviors in our root system (our foundation) and how God can absolutely set us free through the knowledge of His Word. As you read through the story of my life, allow the Holy Spirit to reveal to you any situations in your life that may have planted a seed of fear, doubt, shame, bitterness, or anything that is not of God in your root system and as He reveals, pluck it up and give it to God. Let Him into that area to bring total healing and restoration!

2 Timothy 1:7 says "God has not given us a spirit of fear and timidity, but of power, love and self-discipline."

Father, I ask that as I lay out my messy, chaotic and sometimes ugly story, that You use it to bring freedom to all who read it. I bind every wall, block, or hindrance that may keep anyone from seeing roots in their own lives, and I loose the Holy Spirit to go into the depths of each person to reveal the root systems that don't belong, pull them up, and replace them with Your Truth. I ask that you bring revelation, wisdom, and understanding into every life that picks this book up. It is only through the knowledge of Jesus Christ that we are truly free; help us all to understand that and hunger daily for that knowledge. I declare freedom from all bondage in the life of this reader in Jesus' name. Amen.

Section I:
Fear Lost, Love Won

Chapter 1
Not by Choice

When my mother was pregnant with me, the enemy tried to steal my life. The marriage she was in was not healthy by any means. During this time, she hated her own life and was overwhelmed by the situation, let alone the thought of having another baby. She asked herself, "How am I going to do this?" Early in the first trimester, she began to have some light bleeding, and when she realized she was starting to lose the pregnancy, she immediately went to the doctor. They gave her an injection of Diethylstilbestrol (DES), which was an estrogen medication to keep her from miscarrying. They did warn her that this could cause reproduction problems if the baby (that's me!) was a female. Thankfully, she didn't even have to weigh the negatives: she allowed them to administer it, and here I am today with a call and an anointing that is rare and a full-on threat to hell itself! The reason I am starting here is because I want you to see how the enemy works early in our lives to bring negative seeds into our root system. This is where the seed of rejection was planted in my life. I want you to understand that sometimes, these things in life seem to just happen, many times not by choice.

I believe with all that is in me that God created each of us with a unique purpose and a unique temperament. We are beautiful puzzle pieces that will help carry out His Kingdom mandate on this earth. When all the pieces fit together in unity, His Kingdom culture will be established on earth as it is in heaven. He tells us in His Word, "Before I formed you in the womb I knew you; before you were born I sanctified you..." (Jeremiah 1:5a NKJV), and at times, David had to remind himself of God's words: "For you formed my inward parts; you knitted me together in my mother's womb" (Psalm 139:13 ESV). When the enemy is telling us one thing about ourselves, we need to know what the Word of God says about us. We are known by God. We are unique!

I believe with all my heart that when God began weaving my DNA in my mother's womb, the enemy had already started shaking. He knows when God creates a life that is set apart to be another hard-headed, kingdom warrior on this earth to take him down. Because of this, he tried taking me out before I could draw my first breath...BUT HE LOST!

I was born in Long Beach, California, on August 17, 1976, but I wouldn't be there long. By the time I was two, my parents divorced. Shortly after, my mom moved to Oklahoma, where she eventually remarried. At the young age of three, my temperament was already pretty apparent, and my strong will was already rising up. It was the middle of summer, and I had been given this beautiful fur coat--seriously, a fur coat in the middle of summer—and I was determined to wear it! My mom being the cool mom that she is, allowed me to wear it right then, hood tied around my face and all! This was in the days before seat belts were required. There I was, three years old and standing up in the middle of the front seat with my amazing fur coat on as my mom drove down an old gravel road and BAM...blow out! The car flipped, and I was a rag doll flopping up and down and back and forth...but God had His hand on me once again! My mother told me later in life that the doctors said if I wasn't wearing the fur coat, I may not have lived through that accident. See, I've always been strong-willed, and that's okay, because my strong will is from God!

So many times, we look at strong-willed kids with this mindset that they will never make it in life because they are rebellious and defy authority, but I am here to tell you God created these kids this way, and as parents, we have to learn how to steer that will without breaking the spirit. It takes God to help parents steer these strong-willed kids. Believe me, I know: not only was I a strong-willed child, I also gave birth to one. God knew I needed this strong will in order to carry out my mandate on this earth. It gave me a drive that would one day become a very big part of my freedom walk. Just as we are told to daily put on the armor of God,

I believe that my strong will is an important part of the armor I in particular wear. It's kind of like a personalization of my armor.

Growing up, my mom made sure I knew who Jesus was. My walk with Jesus Christ began at the age of four. I knelt down by my bed and asked Him into my heart. Within that same time frame, I had a dream. In this dream, I was walking through a beautiful garden with Jesus as He held my hand. We both were shoeless; the grass was so green and there were daisies all over. We were just talking, and He reached down, picked me up, and sat me on a rock. He then began to speak into me. He said, "You are chosen by Me, and you will always be Mine. I love you and someday you will live with Me in heaven, but you have things to do first." My biggest takeaway from this dream at four years old was that Jesus did not have any shoes on. My mom tells me now that I woke up crying because of it.

I feel like that dream was symbolic of how I would walk in Jesus' shoes to fulfill His mandate on this earth. This dream impacted me greatly at that young age. All through my life when I would feel like I could never measure up, that dream would come flooding back into my memory; even now, thirty-eight years later, it still seems so real. Starting with this dream and on throughout my childhood, the dreams and visions would continue to get stronger and happen more often. This is where real fear began to enter into my life. The dreams and visions that began to happen night after night felt so real and at times were very scary. Now I understand that God has anointed me with a prophetic seer anointing, which means that He shows me things to come through dreams and visions. Many times, though, especially as children, we are without the knowledge of what this truly is, and we become fearful of the unknown.

    One dream I would have over and over would start with me being in my parents' bed. At the foot of their bed there was a huge window, and in my dream, the curtains would open on their own and I would sit and watch these large white ghosts fly around. Then, suddenly, I would be on a park bench; bomber planes would start flying over, and people would start panicking. I remember being so scared of war, and such a strong fear would come over me that I wouldn't be able to move. In each dream, there was an elderly woman in a hat who would appear out of nowhere and hold my hand, so I wasn't afraid. I do not remember ever exchanging words with her, but I felt safe. Other times, I would wake up and see large black shadows standing over my bed. One time, I was screaming in fear, and my mom ran into the room and said she saw a large black triangle with one eye standing over me. She said she seriously thought I was about to die because of all the dreams and things that I would see. My mom, much like the rest of the church at this time, was not very educated in the spiritual realm. This lack of knowledge is what would lead me later in life to seek answers in the Word. In the between season, this wasn't something that ended, but we will get back to the dreams in the next chapter.

Within this same year, I was sexually molested by a younger uncle on my stepdad's side, and because of this, I was always scared to go to my grandparents' home where he lived. I remember my mom making me sleep in the same room as my brother when we went so that I would feel safe, but I didn't. What would happen if my brother fell asleep and couldn't protect me? This situation also caused some medical problems that I would have to heal from for quite some time. The deep-rooted fear from this experience taunted me for many years. I was afraid of being in a room alone with any man, even those I knew well. As I grew up, I thought I had moved past it, until I had a daughter of my own. I remember days when her uncles would pick her up to go to the store for a soda and panic would rise within me. I knew I could trust them, but the "what ifs" caused a lot of anxiety. When I began to look within myself to find out where the anxiety and fear was coming from, I realized I may have forgotten for a season, but the root was still growing. It had just been exposed.

Do you hear what I am saying? I had not given that moment in my childhood a single thought as I grew up. But what it planted in me was very much alive and waiting for the right moment to expose itself. This fear would come and go as my daughter became more independent, staying with family and such. I wasn't knowledgeable as to how to release this fear; therefore, it was allowed to stay because, to me, it was a normal fear. Our emotions are always tied to something in our belief system. It becomes our choice to allow it or release it.

Throughout my childhood and into the early teen years, my family moved a lot. We had very few long-term homes, and this caused a fear of instability in me. My stepdad was an alcoholic his whole adult life. He would stop drinking for short periods of time but always turned back to it. This brought a lot of chaos into our home. Although my mom did an amazing job of helping my older brother and I feel safe, there was still a lot of fear in our home. Fear of lack was very prominent. Sometimes, we had no clue where our next meal would come from. I remember one time when we were sitting at the table eating crackers and drinking broth, my stepdad walked into the house with beer, cigarettes, and McDonalds. Talk about messed up! Because of his actions, we moved from home to home and town to town, as he either ran from those he cheated or as he looked for work. We lived in a van on Lake Hefner in

Oklahoma City for several months with an occasional hotel stay, along with many other places.

It was scary, yet cool at the same time, which I recently realized is possible. As a child, you look at it and wonder if your life will ever be normal like other people you know, but then my mom always seemed to make our home a home no matter where we were.

As we grow up, we do not realize that the things happening in our lives are actually affecting our character and building personalities that are either healthy or unhealthy. Our "not by choice" experiences can place small seeds of fear, shame, and rejection (among other things) in our lives that take root without us even knowing it. When we allow the Holy Spirit in our lives and begin to read the Word of God, darkness within us is brought to light. The enemy is real, and he has come to steal, kill, and destroy God's children! When we rip out these negative roots, he loses his grip on our lives.

"The thief comes only to steal and kill and destroy; I, Jesus Christ, have come that you may have life, and have it to the full." (John 10:10 NIV)

Chapter 2

The In-Between Seasons – The Lack of Knowledge

Into my young pre-teen years, I continued to have a lot of spiritual experiences. I would see demons in the forms of black shadows walking the halls of my home and at times, yes, I would get up and follow them to see where they were headed. I had nightmare after nightmare and numerous dreams of spiritual encounters, demons, and prophetic insights, all before the age of 13. I knew things before others but wasn't really brave enough to say anything. Because of the lack of knowledge of the prophetic and the spiritual realm in our home, my dreams and the things I knew without being told were just set aside and not really dealt with. This is how the fear was allowed to grow. The lack of knowledge in our lives keeps us from recognizing the enemy's schemes; it keeps us blind and can destroy us.

Hosea 4:6 (NKJV) says, "My people are destroyed for a lack of knowledge," and this is why I want to share my story with you, to help bring knowledge into your life as you seek freedom from the bondage of fear.

I will never forget the dream I had around the age of 14. Jesus and I were riding these beautiful white horses, as if we were going into battle. Then, suddenly, here were my mom and my brother on these black horses running all over the place. Jesus and

I were chasing them down, attempting to catch them. The crazy thing was there was no ground. It was almost as if we were all flying. In my dream, we did not catch them before I woke up. I determined at that age that I better start interceding for my family's lives. I wasn't sure of the meaning at that age, but I have always had a very strong discernment, and it doesn't take much to know the white horses represented good and the black horses were bad. What I did not know at this age was that my life was about to fall apart. The dream was warning me, but the lack of knowledge and understanding kept me from realizing it.

    By this time, fear already had a very tight grip on me. Because of the dreams, I was fearful I was going to lose my family, and I was so fearful of the dark that I couldn't even look out a window without my heart pounding out of my chest. This could partially be my stepdad's fault, though, since he did like to stand outside in the dark and look in our windows with a flashlight held up to his face. He loved to freak us out. I had become so fearful of sleep because of the dreams and visions that I could not fall asleep if I didn't play a cassette tape of one of my pastors preaching messages at night. Then there were nights that I would be scared to play the tapes because I feared something might start talking through it. I'm telling you; my mind could muster up anything fearful!

The summer of my fifteenth birthday, I went to church camp at Oral Roberts University in Tulsa. The camp was called Youth America. I was so tired of living in fear, and I determined that summer that I was done. During one of the evening services, I was feeling pretty confident that I was being set free from fear that week and when I went home, I would be a new person. We began to have a pretty powerful manifestation of God's glory in the room, and when that started, some people started to manifest demons. I had my hands up, tears running down my face, and I heard some commotion beside me. I opened my eyes, and there was this young girl squirming on the ground like a snake. I reached down to pray for her, and she slung her head around and in a man's voice said, "Don't touch me!" I backed away quickly and found myself in a place of paralyzing fear. I was raised in a non-denominational church but had been taught very few things at that point about the spiritual warfare. I knew demons were very real because of my past experiences but had never experienced a manifestation at that level before. It was seriously scary for a fourteen-year-old kid already living a life of fear. Today I look back and think to myself, "Oh, if I could go back now, the devil wouldn't have a chance!"

That night, I went to my dorm room and was praying with a group of friends. I looked up and saw the most beautiful, huge angel wielding a sword in one hand and holding an open Bible in the other. I walked over to look into the open Bible, and all I saw was, "Fear not, for I am with you." I believe this was my first insight into the fact that God did not want me walking in fear. It would be many years before this became a revelation, however.

Chapter 3
Reality of The Spiritual Realm

Little did I know that shortly after my fifteenth birthday, a huge change was about to take place in my life. I experienced something I never imagined, but through it all, I learned how real the enemy is and how much I had to cling to God to make it through this life.

We were sophomores in high school, doing what sophomores do on Halloween night...stupid stuff to make you even more scared. I still haven't figured out why it is so fun to purposefully terrify yourself. Anyway, my very best friend and I, along with her boyfriend, were going on a haunted hayride. Before the ride you had an option to go into the barn and see a "fortune teller." I had enough teaching and enough spiritual background to know this was not a wise idea. Unfortunately, my best friend and her boyfriend refused to listen; they just wanted to see if they were going to get married. So, they went in. When they came back out, they were pretty shaken up. I asked, "Did she say you were going to break up or something?" They replied, "No, all she kept seeing was glass and fire. But what does she know? It's just kid stuff anyway." As teenagers do, we blew it off and went on the hayride. What we didn't realize is that fortune tellers, psychics, mediums, or whatever else you call them, are tools the enemy uses to speak curses over God's children. The Word of God tells us there is life and death in the power of our tongue. True prophets of God speak LIFE, but those we would call "false" prophets speak curses, death, and destruction—to put it shortly, the lies of the enemy. This puts word curses on those receiving it. It is very clear in the Word that we are to stay away from such people.

"There shall not be found among you anyone who makes his son or his daughter pass through the fire, one who practices witchcraft, or a soothsayer, or one who interprets omens, or a sorcerer, or one who conjures spells, a medium, or a spiritist, or one who calls up the dead." (Deuteronomy 18:10-11 NKJV)

Two weeks later on November 17, we would face the most horrific, life-changing tragedy any fifteen-year-old kid or parent would want to face. My best friend and her boyfriend were killed in a tragic car accident. They were driving at a high rate of speed crossing a mile-long bridge. As they got to the other side of the bridge, they had a blowout, ping-ponged from side to side, and the pick-up truck stopped as it wrapped around a tree, shattering all the glass on the vehicle and exploding into flames. They were pinned in the truck, and no one could get to them because the flames were so intense.

This changed me forever. In a dream, I woke up in the middle of the night before her funeral, and she came walking into my room. I cried and tried to hold her, and she wouldn't let me. She just looked at me and said, "I'm okay. I'm very happy where I am, and I want you to stop crying over me. Please live your life to the fullest." Then she was gone. I was so angry at God because I thought He allowed her death to happen. I remember crying out and telling God I didn't want to see that stuff anymore. No more dreams, no more visions, NO MORE ANYTHING! Little did I know, this was an amazing seer anointing and prophetic gift that I was asking Him to remove. I was allowing the enemy to twist the gift of God in my life through fear, and I chose to lay it down. We have to be so careful about the inner vows that we speak. When we ask God to remove something, He will.

I know at this point you are probably thinking, "what a dark and horrible life," right? Are you wondering why on earth I am sharing such details of my life with you? Because, my friend, I do not want you to suffer through life without the knowledge of how real the spiritual realm is. I don't want to see any other anointed men and women of God laying down their kingdom gifts because they are too fearful to move forward. FEAR IS A LIAR, and IN CHRIST, WE HAVE VICTORY! Once I realized that fear was the driving force behind many of my choices, I chose to repent for asking God to take the seer anointing from my life, and I asked Him to restore it. He is a faithful God!

Another reason I'm sharing this particular story with you is because I want you to also see how real the demonic is, how the enemy can go in and through the mouths of others who speak word curses over us. We have to stop playing with the devil and start using our God-given authority against him. Had I known the truth of how the enemy works on October 31, 1991, I would have rebuked those very words the psychic spoke over them and declared the power of Holy Spirit life. We need more education in the churches on false prophets (mediums, psychics, witches, soothsayers, horoscopes, etc.) and false teachers (religion created by false doctrine). The Word of God is very clear that we are not to take part in any of that stuff. All you have to do is read 1 and 2 Peter to see that!

If you have found yourself seeking for answers through any source but God, then I encourage you to renounce that in your life! Renounce simply means to formally declare one's abandonment of claim, right or possession. When we allow these things in our lives, spiritually we lay claim on what the false prophet says, which means we give the enemy the right to come in and lay claim on us. When we renounce it, we are letting the enemy know he no longer has a hold on us through that bad choice.

Here's an example of how you can renounce those other sources:

"Father, I come before you in the name of Jesus Christ, my Lord and Savior. I ask that You forgive me for allowing fear to drive my life. I ask that You forgive me for seeking other sources to guide me because of my own ignorance of the Truth. I renounce __(what you chose to dabble in)__ in my life, and I promise to not turn to any other source but You from this day forward. Now I bind every demonic spirit that has attached itself into my life through these means of guidance, and I loose the Holy Spirit, the Spirit of Truth, into my life to guide my every footstep. For Your Word is a lamp unto my feet and a light unto my path (Psalm 119:105). Thank You, Father, for freedom! In Jesus' name, amen.

This small dent in the history of my life is exactly that, a small dent. But let me tell you this, these small dents can lock us in a place of spiritual bondage that without God we will never get past. Then enemy's goal is to keep us so bound that we lose sight of our identity in Christ. This is exactly what happened to me. Fear stole my identity!

Chapter 4
The Year of God's Grace

The summer after my best friend was killed, I began to spiral down and was quickly losing my God-breathed identity. I pulled away from God quite a bit. I was becoming more rebellious; I was angry at God still, and I just wanted to live how I wanted to live. I began dating the "bad" boys. I was so drawn to them, partially because I thought I could fix them and partially because I got tired of being the "church" girl. I had many crushes between the ages of fourteen and sixteen, but none of them would date me because they knew my morals. One in particular refused to date me because I was "too pure" for him. I got tired of that for a little while, but I look back and thank God that He is the one that protected me and held me up. I had my first boyfriend that summer. I was head over heels because someone finally wanted to date the "church" girl with morals. Little did I know, he wasn't dating me because he liked me as much as I liked him. He had actually made a bet with another friend that he could take my virginity. I had never really even kissed a boy before; I for sure wasn't going that far! I had promised God my purity until marriage, and no one was getting it. After four months of dating, he began to get a little pushy with me, and I began to pull away. I felt so important when I was with him, but I knew I couldn't let down my boundaries. Finally, I had to break up with him because he began to get angry with me for saying no. God knew what was best and He had another plan.

I turned sixteen in August and broke up with my boyfriend in September; in October, I met the man that God would use to bring transformation in my life. Being raised with an alcoholic father, his addiction didn't just affect him; it affected his family and many more in his sphere of influence. My mom and my stepdad divorced when I was thirteen, and I became pretty fearful of loss. I first lost him, then my best friend, and this caused some negative roots in my life. I became a controlling approval addict who feared rejection, and full-blown timidity set in. The once outspoken, adventurous, and brave girl turned into a quiet, timid, withdrawn ball of chains. The cool thing is that God will use other people as tools to bring healing into our lives. If we are willing vessels, then He's a willing God.

God brought Abraham into my life during a very vulnerable and angry season. I remember I was just running amok. I stopped going to church because my family stopped going. Remember my dream at fourteen? God had already been warning me of this season. I stepped away from my dreams because fear totally overtook me. Every once in a while, I would get a glimpse of that dream from when I was four, and God would remind me that I was chosen by Him. He was just waiting.

I was a sixteen-year-old girl who was lost, hurting, angry, and lonely. Thankfully, Abraham had the perfect temperament and heart of mercy to handle this girl. I met him in October 1992; he was twenty-two (one-month shy of twenty-three), and I was a fresh sixteen. WOW!

Thinking back, that sounds absolutely crazy, but God had a plan. Our first date was October 31 – one year to the day my best friends stepped into a fortune teller's barn, and the enemy placed a curse on their lives. Two weeks later, November 15, we would celebrate his twenty-third birthday, taking my focus off of the first anniversary of their death. God is so strategic when you really stop to think about it. At the time, I didn't really think about God being in it, but I now know He was all up in my business.

Abraham became my life, my reason for waking up every day with hopes of getting to see his face or hear his voice at least once. I was still pretty withdrawn from many of the friends I had from before my best friend's death, but I felt like I was alive again every time I was with him. I felt loved and protected. I knew my life would be okay as long as he was in it.

Before I met Abraham, there were days I would go and lay on my best friend's grave and just cry. I was so alone and felt so abandoned. But because God has always carried me in the palm of

His hand, He knew exactly who I needed in that exact moment. He knew exactly who I needed in my life to help me become who He created me to be. Throughout that first year of our relationship, my deep hurt began to be replaced with love again. It was a year of healing for me—healing from the loss so that I could love and live again. But it proved to be a long road for me to learn to receive love and live love because of all of the deep roots in my foundational belief system. Throughout my older teen years, I was very stubborn, to the point that I HATED—let me repeat—HATED being corrected. If someone corrected me, I would cut them off and go the opposite direction. My fear of rejection and abandonment turned into a really low self-esteem, which in turn caused me to become very defensive. I was a spoiled brat! NO LIE! And have I mentioned strong-willed? I look back today and wonder how on earth Abraham had the patience that he did with me! This was a year that, through him, God's grace just poured out on me.

My fear of everything caused a lot of mistakes and damage in the beginning of our relationship. When we experience great loss through death, divorce, or betrayal, it opens the door to a spirit of abandonment, leaving us with a fear of being alone or left behind. If we allow this to fester for too long, this spirit will take up residency within our soul, and we will look at everyone through this distorted lens. They will do one thing that triggers it, and immediately, we will fall into this cycle over and over, believing that they too may abandon us.

    This leads to a very lonely life, and it is one based in fear! When we experience these things, we need to be quick to forgive and allow the grieving process to be completed in our lives. We can't get stuck in any stage of life because this is where it festers. One of the best ways I look at these kinds of situations now is that it may be crushing at the moment, but what new wine will God bring forth in the end? Please don't allow yourself to get stuck like I did!

Chapter 5
The Identity Thief

Since the beginning of time, the enemy has attempted to confuse our God-breathed identity. When you look all the way back to Adam and Eve, that was exactly his plot. Let's look at the story: In Genesis 1 and 2, we are told about the absolutely beautiful garden God created for mankind. God said, "Let Us (Father, Son, Holy Spirit) make man in Our image (a triune being – Spirit, soul and body), according to Our likeness..." So, God created man in His own image; in the image of God, He created him; male and female, He created them (Genesis 1:26-27 KNJV). When you look at this passage of scripture, you see that we are created in the image of God. Our identity is found IN HIM and no one else. But the enemy came in as a deceitful serpent and made Eve question her identity.

In Genesis 3, the serpent was more crafty and cunning than any beast of the field which the Lord God had made. He said to the woman, "Has God indeed said, 'You shall not eat of every tree of the garden'?" and the woman said, "We may eat of the fruit of the trees of the garden; but the fruit of the tree which is in the midst of the garden, God said, 'You shall not eat it, nor shall you touch it, lest you die.'" The enemy began to argue with her, telling her that she isn't going to "die" per se, but when she does eat of it, she will become "like God, knowing good and evil." What a deceptive lie.

No, she wasn't going to immediately die a physical death, but she would die a spiritual death because she questioned her identity and sin entered into her life, bringing a separation between humans and God. She ate and immediately her natural eyes were opened, and her spiritual eyes were closed.

This is how the enemy so deceptively comes into our lives through circumstances, people, loss, hurt, anger, bitterness, shame, guilt, and so much more. We fall prey believing that it's just an emotion when all the while, he's planting seeds that will take root in those of us without knowledge of the Truth. Eve had knowledge but not full Truth. She heard secondhand from Adam what God commanded; then, she repeated something different, and it gave the enemy a foothold in her life. All of the deceptions I mentioned above lie in the strongman of fear. This fear is what comes in and takes our identity.

I knew from a young age that God called me. He told me in dreams, many of them. He spoke it through the mouths of prophets, and He's put a passion in me that many don't experience. But because of the enemy's lies and the fear that I lived in, I was much older before I was truly able to step into my place in the Kingdom. I questioned many times who I really was. I did not see myself created in His image. This is something that I want to see end! I want to see spiritual freedom from young to old, a freedom that breaks the chains of bondage and sets the captives free! It is a freedom that His children are supposed to be walking in because it's our mandate to be the chain breakers, not the ones in the chains.

"Before I formed you in the womb I knew you; before you were born, I set you apart..." Jeremiah 1:5 (NIV)

"Those He predestined [that's us], He also called; those He called, He also justified; those He justified, He also glorified. What then, shall we say to these things? If God is for us, who can be against us?" Romans 8:30-31 (NKJV)

God created you for a purpose. He created you in His image; He formed you, called you, and chose you! Like I said before, the truth of who we are is found IN HIM, not in the things against us. The enemy, though, is dumb enough to keep trying.

Chapter 6

The Thief Comes to Steal, Kill, and Destroy

Abraham and I married on March 12, 1994, at the end of my senior year of high school. It started off as wonderfully as we expected. I finished high school while he worked, and everything was going great. Right out of high school, I went to work as the secretary in a tire shop next door to the dealership where he worked. We just knew we had entered the fairytale life: I had found the perfect man; we owned a home, a farm, and cattle; and we loved life. That fairytale quickly came to an end toward the end of June 1994. Remember, "The thief comes only to steal and kill and destroy..." John 10:10 (NIV).

Abraham had been having stomach trouble for several months. We went to doctors but had not received any solid answers. I won't go into the details of all of those doctor appointments, but because no doctor would take the stomach pain seriously, they chose not to really treat him. This ended with a major bang! One morning, he collapsed, and after final tests at a local doctor, he was rushed to the hospital with a perforated stomach. He had a hole the size of a half dollar in his stomach lining, and his entire abdominal cavity was filled with air and days-old foods he had eaten. He had emergency surgery within hours of the diagnosis. Eight days and over $100,000.00 in medical bills later, we were two lost newlyweds with no clue where to even start again. I was seventeen and just out of high school with no training for any profession yet; he was a GM Technician, but he couldn't work for weeks. Fear over our finances (not having enough to live) and the fear of losing my husband to premature death overwhelmed me daily. This led to some very controlling behavior again. I wanted to control every part of his life because I knew how to keep him healthy and alive, or so I thought. I forgot that God knew more than both of us. I had to learn through the ups and the downs that God will take care of what concerns me. It's not my place to control anyone or the outcome of their decisions.

God placed Abraham in my life for a very specific purpose, and the enemy knew this! His goal was to destroy my husband, add fuel to my fears, and possibly destroy me. Remember, Abraham was my life. My belief was that there was no way at that point in my life that I could have gone on without him. This was a fear and control struggle that I would face for years to come. I look back today and wish I would have had someone in my life to grab me by the face and say, "LISTEN!! If you could stop living a life of panic and chaos during negative situations and start pausing long enough to say, 'God, what's the purpose of this attack?', you would realize that the victory is already yours and you would be able to fight from a victorious stance." Of course, this is coming from the me I am twenty-five years later, but my desire is to see you free and victorious early in the fight rather than years down the road.

After overcoming that major obstacle, I began to have some reproductive problems. I saw a few doctors, and the bottom line of the diagnosis was infertility. I was told that I had a disease called endometriosis and if I did not have my kids by the time I was 20, it would be nearly impossible for me to have children. My uterus was already showing signs of the disease. Remember me telling you earlier the medication my mom was given could cause reproductive complications for the "female" later in life? Well, my doctor even went as far as to tell me that IF I did become pregnant that I wouldn't be able to carry the baby to term. My heart was broken. I wanted a baby; I always had since I was young. In fact, I wanted four! Although we were not about to start having kids while I was still seventeen, we chose at that time to leave it in God's hands. But I still was being fed lies as the enemy whispered in my ear year after year, "You aren't good enough to produce natural children." A year later, I miscarried at a very early stage of pregnancy. In all honesty, I did not know I was pregnant until the miscarriage happened, and the doctor informed me. I was heartbroken, but I also suddenly had hope because I was able to get pregnant; however, the fear of not being able to carry it still taunted me. That being said, we know

Jesus is a life giver and the revelation of that would soon become very real to me!

Jesus said, "I have come that they may have life, and have it to the full" John 10:10 (NIV).

Before this time, I had not really gotten back into church. We attended church for the sake of good works, but our relationship with God was not there. I knew in my heart that God had promised me that I would be a mother, so at this point I began searching out the Word again. I began to seek God like I knew I was supposed to. I came to the realization that I had forgotten my first love. It would be a few years before I became pregnant, but I knew God would be faithful to fulfill His promises in my life. In the winter of 1996, I found out that I was pregnant. I felt as if I was pregnant forever, as she was born at FORTY-ONE WEEKS ... so much for the "you can't carry to term" words. She was a whopping 8lb 10oz and 22.5 inches long. She was perfect in every way.

Through the attack on my husband's health and my daughter's birth, I became very interested in the medical field. So, when she was 4 months old, I left my job and started nursing school. This was a journey that opened up so many doors for me and probably the first step to me learning that fear can't rule every aspect of my life. I was confident in my nursing skills, very well taught, and I did it to the best of my ability. For many years, this would be the only area that I was able to walk into fearlessly.

In 2001, I became pregnant with my son. This pregnancy proved to be pretty difficult, so I had to leave my job at the hospital. After months of hospital visits and bedrest due to preterm labor, he was born four weeks early and was still 8lbs 3 oz and 21.5 inches long. He had a lot of health problems, as most pre-term babies do, and we almost lost him when he was six weeks old because he had severe acid reflux and aspirated in his sleep. I woke up around 3 am to him, blue in the face and gurgling in his bed. By this time, I was a nurse, and thank God I knew what to do. For the next year, we had a lot of doctor visits, tests, and fear that kept me from sleeping many nights! I feared I would wake up in the morning to a child not breathing. This is a fear that will taunt you like no other.

Both of my kids have a very strong call of God on their lives. I know this for a fact because in human terms, they aren't even supposed to be here, and looking back, I can see how God has preserved them for such a time as this! At the time of this writing, our daughter is twenty-one, and our son is eighteen years old. They may not see their full purpose yet, but they do know they are called and chosen. Now it's up to them to choose yes.

Do you see how the enemy attempted to literally destroy the lives of my family? He does this to all of us using different methods, but we must learn to recognize his tactics. Know that he does nothing new under the sun; he only repeats the same things over and over.

Chapter 7

The Healing Begins Through Obedience

"Many are the plans in a man's heart, nevertheless the Lord's counsel – purpose – will stand." (Proverbs 19:21 NKJV)

From 1994 to 2004, we lived in the small town of Lookeba, Oklahoma. We owned our home and owned a farm. Abraham was a mechanic by day and farmer by night and weekends, and I was working as a nurse. Life was better but still not stable in many ways. In 2000, I told Abraham that we needed to find a spirit-filled church because I didn't want my kids raised in a church not teaching the entire Word of God. We ventured out across the street from our house where we met some amazing pastors, and God introduced Abraham to the experience of what it means to be non-denominational. Our hunger for God grew and grew, and we both wanted as much as we could get. We served and we studied for three years, and at the end of 2003, God began to lay on our hearts to move 1200 miles away from anything and everyone we knew. We knew it was God and we were hungry for more of Him, so we said YES to the call! In the beginning of 2004, we started the process of leaving our local church and began preparing for the move. During this time, we visited the church I grew up in, The Rock of Restoration Church. It was only a few weeks before we were set to go; we were there on a Sunday morning, and during worship, I felt these hands touch my shoulders.

As I opened my eyes, there was this blonde woman standing a little too close for my comfort levels and staring me straight in the face. She began to prophesy over me about breaking women free from chains of bondage. She told me that I was to be a light to all I influenced and so much more. I was in awe because I knew what God had told me, but the only other people who knew were our pastors, who were not there, and my husband, who doesn't talk to many people. I knew it was confirmation from God. I never got her name; she just finished speaking and walked away. I would wonder for many years who this amazing prophetess was. In the midst of the first few months of 2004, we sold everything, packed up our six-year-old and three-year-old and everything we could fit in a 21-foot cargo trailer, and we took off to a land unknown!

This, my friends, was the beginning of a new era in our lives! Never again would we be the same four people who left Oklahoma to explore the coastal shores of Savannah, Georgia. God had a plan that man knew not of. God is in the life wrecking, restoring and transforming business, and this is what happened to us for the next seven years. On June 7, 2004, we pulled into Savannah, GA. We had no jobs, no home, no church, no friends, nothing... well, nothing but a call from God. Within five days, Abe had an AMAZING job, we found a home, and God was about to lead us to a church called "Bethesda." This was our healing ground for the next season of our lives.

By this time in my life, I knew God had called me to ministry; remember, it had been prophesied by the unknown woman, and Jesus told me when I was four years old. I had no clue what that looked like at the time, but I thought I did! The day I walked into that church; I held my head so high that it almost fell off backwards. Boy, did I have a spirit of pride inside of me! Pride is fed by fear, remember that. I tease now and say when I walked in, I was thinking in my head, "You have no clue who just walked through your doors!" Seriously, that was my mindset. My sweet friend, Vanessa Hicks, teasingly told me a few years later as we were taking counseling courses together, "I couldn't tell that first day that you walked in here whether you knew it all or whether you knew nothing at all!" We laughed, of course, but it was the truth! I replied, "I knew nothing at all!" God used the people in that body to begin a process in me that has never ended, and I pray never does!

I continued to walk in all these fears, even though I showed a very confident façade. I was so scared no one was going to like me. I feared rejection so badly that I would leave events before anyone even had the chance to reject me. Those who suffer from a fear of rejection will usually reject others before anyone has the chance to reject them. One life-changing moment for me was about 8 months after we moved there. I was at a women's night, and when it was over, all the women kind of grouped together, and I felt left out. I decided quickly that this wasn't for me, so I gathered my things and headed to my car. I have no clue where this man came from but standing by my car was the pastor of the church.

He asked, "Where are you going?" and I quickly replied "Home!" He then went on to say, "You know God has placed you here for a purpose. You know the call you have on your life. Now, you have two choices here: 1. You leave now, and a year from now, you are still in the same place you are today, no friends and not moving forward, or 2. You can go back in there, get in the crowd and get to know some people, and a year from now, you will see a lot of change." Needless to say, I chose option number two. This was a huge step for me. I was facing a fear that I hadn't put myself in a position to face before this. I was going to "invite" myself into a group of women I did not know. WOW! It still took years for that fear to be broken, but I am not one to purposefully

stay stagnant in my walk with God. It has happened but only accidentally.

Shortly after this, I was approached by a counseling student who asked if I would be willing to help her get her degree by taking an Arno Profile System questionnaire. I agreed, and in those few short visits, I discovered my purpose, my heart, my passion, and the fears I was allowing to control me. I also realized I needed RESTORATION! I wanted to be someone who helps others restore their lives back to God's original plans for them, to help them get rid of the confusion and chaos of life's situations, personally chosen or put upon them by others, and bring them to a place of wholeness in Christ Jesus. Therefore, I started school to be a counselor.

We were in Georgia for seven years, and God did some absolutely amazing things in our lives! He broke pride in me, he broke the fears of being corrected and confronted off of me, and he broke my people-pleasing mentality. I still had a TON to walk through and heal from, but this was a huge beginning for me. There was so much healing that came forth in that short seven-year span. I want you to hear this: sometimes, God asks us to do things—big things that take a lot of faith. It's in our yes that we will see His hand move. To walk in faith in the truth of His Word is where freedom comes from. Faith in combination with our works is needed to be kingdom minded.

Chapter 8
Fear Still Owned Me

The strongest fear I carried was the fear of man, more specifically, people's thoughts toward me. This fear kept me paralyzed and running from my dreams instead of to them. It owned me. When something keeps you from pursing your purpose, it's being allowed ownership of your life. I knew this had to change, but I didn't know how.

In April 2011, we decided to move back to Oklahoma in order to help care for Abraham's parents, as they were beginning to face some health issues. This return was one of the hardest decisions I've ever had to make. We had made some very close friends in Georgia, and God had knitted our hearts together with many in our church. Although the last year there was a difficult year with relationships changing and things being realigned, it was still hard to leave. God used the positive and negative experiences at our church to teach me many things I was to use in my current season. At the time, though, all I felt was hurt, more rejection, and more disappointment from which I would have to heal. We had people we did life with for years stop speaking to us completely because we moved. They felt we were making a wrong decision, so they chose to cut us off. That was painful. Our family needed us, and we were making the best decision we could for our immediate and extended family. I have learned over the years that not everyone will accept the decisions you feel God wants in your personal life, and it's okay.

As I mentioned before, this sent me back to Oklahoma not only angry that we had to leave but also with some added fears to deal with, which I did not recognize until much later. Little did I know at the time that God had such a huge purpose in moving us back to Oklahoma! He has a mandate on my life that couldn't be fulfilled where we were; instead, He had to have us here in the beautiful town of Weatherford, Oklahoma. We arrived July 7, 2011, on what I believe was the hottest day recorded in the history of the town. On top of that, it was a summer of sandstorms and severe drought. I argued with God for over a year: "ARE YOU SERIOUS? You took me from the beautiful, green grass of Georgia, where it rains daily and it's never too hot? You took me from the beach for this??? FOR THIS???" Why would He do this to me? I just wanted to move back! I was angry and wanted nothing to do with "new" people, ministry, church, or life in Weatherford.

I will never forget the first time I visited the church we now call home! We left, and I told my husband, "that's not Bethesda, and I don't like it." I stayed home many Sunday's watching my Georgia church family online while Abraham would attend the local church. I'm not lying when I say I was angry. I laid down my desires to do ministry, counsel, and serve God wholeheartedly, and I went back to work as a nurse. I was done! I will never forget my mom coming for a visit, and as she left, she looked at me and asked, "What happened to my little girl that had a dream to counsel and serve in ministry?" I looked at her very daringly and said, "She's gone!" Do you see that spirit of fear working? Fear of the unknown, rejection, abandonment?

I honestly do not remember much of that year, but I do believe that my anger was rooted in the fear of the unknown, which I wasn't used to experiencing since I've always been a bit daring. I have fought a lot of fear, but I still had quite an adventurous nature. This time, though, was different. I felt shame, and I feared I made a big mistake leaving Georgia and that my purpose was there. I feared that I missed the boat, so to speak. I feared that I would never taste of that desire to just DO for Him like I had there. I feared I was out of His will and there was no way to return. In all that fear, I ran even further away, and the fear was fueling the run. I remember thinking I might as well just quit because I missed it big time with this move. I held so much fear! There is no fear like the fear that you've let down God. It took me a few years to realize that is not possible. I am reminded of this in Philippians 1:6, "… He who began a good work in you will carry it to completion." God does not start something without finishing it, and when we feel like it's over but our heart is still for His purpose, we need to remember we serve a God who is so faithful, a God who reminds us once again, "No weapon formed against you shall prosper and if He is for us then who on earth can be against us?!? FEAR NOT, for I am with you!" The enemy's weapon of fear in my life was about to be broken.

Chapter 9

The Turn Around

In 2013, there was a major turnaround for me. It was my birthday weekend, and Dr. Tim Byler, our Pastor from Georgia, showed up. Oh my gosh, I was so excited! I was excited because I just knew in his prophetic way, he was going to tell us it was time to come home. Only, nope, no, he didn't! To my surprise, he corrected me; in fact, he loves to correct me. He was the one that God used to break that fear of correction off of me. He hadn't changed a bit in two years when we saw him again, because he was still correcting me.

He sat me down and explained to me that it was time for me to let go of Georgia. God had sent him here to release me and tell me to move on. Of course, I cried and argued, but he so kindly explained that our season there is complete, and we won't be moving back. He told me I needed to let go of anger and move forward. Move forward? That meant making new friends and letting people back into my life, which to me was not only a no but a heck no! I know the pattern there, and I wasn't willing to open back up.

My excuse was this: "I am melancholy by nature. God created me that way, and that means that I don't like being pushed into unfamiliar things. I don't like being told what to do, and I for sure don't like being around people I don't know!" Over the next several years, however, I learned that's not my Fathers' heart, and *I'm not as introverted as fear has kept me.* Before he left for Georgia, Tim asked me to promise him one thing: that I would go on the women's trip with our church ladies to Joyce Meyers that next month. Of course, it would just happen to be advertised the Sunday he comes to our church—Of course it would! I made up every excuse from "I don't have the money" to "I can't take off work," but he not only made ME promise, he made Abraham promise, too. "Oh," I thought, "Now you're turning my husband against me! Nice one! Nice one!" I remember asking my boss the day before I left if he was absolutely sure that he didn't need me there because I was more than willing to stay home. He looked me straight in the eyes and said, "No, go and enjoy yourself!" UUUGGGGHHHH, even he wouldn't help me. The fear of man and the unknown was ruling my life. I just wanted to go back to the familiar, but I have learned that God loves to push us into the unfamiliar.

    Well, as you may have guessed, it's September 2013, and I'm stuck in a Suburban, driving two days with a bunch of women I don't know. In all honesty, I was scared to death. What if they didn't like me? What if I said something that made someone mad (have I mentioned I don't filter myself when I'm talking well, either?)? What if? What if? What if? Fear was speaking big time!

God used this trip to teach me that I am loved and that there are people out there who love without measure and with whom there is no judgment. I made so many new friends on that trip, and God proved Himself over and over! I couldn't tell you to this day what a single speaker spoke, and I couldn't tell you a single song we sang, but I can tell you the amazing conversations we had in our rooms, while waiting in line in the horrible heat, and while sharing amazing meals. It was amazing. The turnaround was coming!

The life-changing part came once I arrived home. I went to bed that night and had a spiritual encounter that I have never had before. I will do my best to explain it. It was all my fears wrapped up in one solid night. I got into bed around 10:30 pm, and I rolled over onto my right side. As I began to fall asleep, I felt something brush up against my back. I turned over to look, and as I lay on my back, a black shadow, which I believe was a demonic spirit, laid on top of me and pretty much held me in place, locked to my bed from 10:45 pm until 6:30 am. I would go in and out of this insane nightmare. The nightmare started with the same dream I had over and over as a child. I was sitting on a park bench and airplanes began to fly over and drop bombs. Everyone was running in panic, and a little lady with a white hat would appear and take my hand and make me feel safe. Then, I was in an old house, and the lady in the white hat was in a back room glaring at me down the hall. Massive fear overtook me at this point. I tried to walk out onto my back porch, but we were on the edge of this ocean, and the waves were black and HUGE and about to take out the house. Then, I heard, "I'm going to have your children." I ran back in and saw my husband. The really strange thing was the anger I was feeling in this dream. It was unbearable; I was screaming and cussing, and it was not me at all. I kept thinking, "If I can get to Abraham, he will wake me up, and this will be over," but when I yelled for him, he said, "I don't know you; you're not the same person!" I woke up for a moment still locked down on my bed, then went back into another nightmare. The anger in every scenario was absolutely overpowering, and the threats to take out my family even worse. The anger was an anger that you would feel before killing someone, like life-threatening anger.

Abraham's alarm went off at 6:30 am, and immediately, the spirit lifted and I could move. I sat up in the bed and just started bawling. I was ugly crying. I couldn't stop. I kept saying to Abraham, "You wouldn't help me! You ran from me all night long," and he was a bit freaked out because he didn't realize what was going on. I ended up missing work that day because I couldn't mentally function. I was an absolute mess.

I ended up texting the dream to my friend's husband, and immediately he came back with, "I don't know what happened this weekend, but whatever it was, you pissed the devil off!" (I'm quoting him exactly here, so don't judge!) All I did was attend a women's conference. How does that make the devil mad? I didn't even remember what the speakers said. Wait a minute... I suddenly remembered a conversation I had with my roommate and now awesome friend, Amy. She explained to me that our church did not have a women's ministry that met often. She mentioned that the only thing the women did was go to Joyce in St. Louis every year. In response to that, I replied, "Well, I will NEVER do that again!" She, being the prodder that she is, began asking all kinds of nosy questions, then went on to tell me that I should start a women's ministry here. "OH, HECK NO!" were my thoughts, but I did promise her I would think about it. I planned to think on that for a long time in hopes she would forget! You see, I had attempted to lead women's ministries since I was called into the ministry in 2003, and none of them were very successful, so to protect myself and my pride, I allowed the fear of failure and man to keep me in a pit of comfort! I was not doing it! Nope! No way!

    I found myself in my Pastor's office that afternoon to talk about this dream/nightmare I had. I wanted to get another opinion and make sure I didn't have an anger demon or something in me. I'm telling you, that anger was unreal, and I just knew it was God showing me I had a problem! But after sharing this dream with my Pastor, his response was the same as my friend's husband: "I don't know what happened this weekend, but you've ticked the devil off. The anger you were feeling was his anger; the threats against your family are to keep you in fear and not move forward!" Well, I can honestly say I had not been moving forward for two years. That explained why the enemy had been so quiet in my life. I was exactly where he wanted me.

Well, far be it for me to let the devil have his way! This is where my strong will comes in handy, like I told you it would! I turned to my Pastors and said, "Well, if my weekend trip made him mad, then let's just finish it off. Will you two pray about allowing me to step in to lead a women's ministry here?"

Immediately, they both said, "YES! We do not need to pray about this!" I then said to myself, "What the heck did you just do? Did you just seriously ask to step back into ministry!?!" I wanted to bang my head against a wall over and over. Fear gripped me instantly. I am not kidding. I left their office and went home immediately. I told my husband about our meeting and then about what I asked them. He looked at me with his "big-eyed" look and had no words. The interpretation of that is, "What in the world were you thinking!?!?" I responded with a loud, "I know! I have no clue what I just did. I need to call them and let them know I can't do it. I've changed my mind." I thought I was going to throw up. He encouraged me to pray about it and go to bed to sleep on it and not make another decision that day. I agreed.

Let's fast forward a few months. As I prepared to meet with the women for the first time, I was nauseous, I was so fearful, and I wanted to tuck tail and run the other direction! We had our first meeting scheduled for December 2013, but the weather was bad, so we cancelled! That was the best day of my month. I was rejoicing deep inside. Why? Because I was so full of fear. What if no one liked me, what if I stumbled over my words (which I still do today, but it's all good! We're all used to it!), what if no one even showed up!?! Oh, I was so scared! Well, for a few weeks I had peace, but when the new date arrived, January 2014, all the negative emotions began to flow again. I told my husband, "I can't do this. I'm going to tell them I made a mistake. I quit." The funny thing was that he really didn't argue with me, probably because he knows me too well and knew that my mind would change sooner or later.

This is where my husband is my strength. He told me many years ago that he believed God called me. He has been my bulldozer, so to speak; he has pushed me when I didn't think I could do it. He encourages me and is always letting me know that he believes in the call on my life. In our twenty-five years of marriage, he has never discouraged me from moving forward unless it was just a bad idea, and for those times, I am very thankful. He prays over me, speaks greatness into me, and never lets me speak death into the dream inside of me. He helps push me through my fears, and he has helped me become the bold, confident, courageous woman I am today. Like I said earlier, God knew exactly who I needed in my life to help me become who He created me to be. I should point out, though, that this only works because we understand what it means to be submitted to God and submitted to each other.

With him pushing me forward, I led the women's ministry at our church for two years while walking in fear and doubt. With every meeting I was nauseous and wanted to quit because I just hated it. Yet, I didn't. It was so weird! It was the worst love/hate relationship ever. I would do all the planning but find other people to speak, or we would do fellowship events, so I didn't have to be in front of people. If I did end up speaking, I was a hot mess for over 24 hours before and 48 hours after! What I have learned is that when we are walking in fear, we cannot be fully released to be who God has created us to be. When we are walking in fear, we constantly compare, compete, doubt, and get offended at the smallest things.

Have you ever looked at yourself one way, but when you get in front of a group of people, you become something totally different? For example, let's say you see yourself as this courageous, on fire, prophetic lioness that's full of power and the Word, but when you get in front of people, you all of a sudden become timid, quiet, weak and unable to remember any part of the Word? Yep, that's me, right here! I have learned since writing this book that fear hinders the anointing of God in our lives. God anointed me to do a mighty work: He has placed on me the mantle of a general (apostle) with the anointing of a prophet and teacher but because of fear, I would freeze every time I stood in front of people. This kept me from fully flowing in the anointing.

Fear and anointing do not mix!

Chapter 10
The Release

In early 2015, one of my best friends texted me and said, "My husband and I were praying for you this morning. As we were praying, I saw a vision of you so bound. You were bound with chains and a crown of thorns on your head with blood running down. I heard God say, 'I just need her to surrender.'" I responded with an irritated, "How on earth do I surrender? I don't even know what that looks like." Her response back was, "Good question!"

I am one of those people who needs to see the picture. I want to see what something looks like so that I have a goal to reach. I thought I had fully surrendered. I mean, I was doing exactly what God wanted me to, right? After that text, I felt more confused than I had been before. I left for work and thought on it all day long. Here's a peculiar yet cool thing about God: you do not need to see everything He wants done in your life. You may not have a clue what it looks like, but He has it all planned. He just needs us to trust Him in the process.

A few weeks later, January 25, 2015, to be exact, I was in church service, and during worship, I began to ask God, "What does surrender truly mean?" I needed to know because I was so tired of being bound. All I could see when I closed my eyes to worship was the image my friend had given me from her vision during prayer. I didn't want to see it anymore. I will never forget; it was the third song, "Our God Is Greater."

Pastor Marquieta was singing, and she began to quote Romans 8:31: "If God is for us, who can be against us?" As she began to prophesy, I lost all strength in my legs. I fell to my knees, and as I did, I literally saw in the spirit chains shattering, pieces of them flying everywhere. Now before this moment, NO ONE in my church had seen me cry! Up until this moment, I didn't cry much. But let me tell you this, as I saw those chains shatter, I began to weep, and I was once again U-G-L-Y crying. It was a freedom cry! I had lost all concept of time, place, and what dignity I thought I had. As I was on the ground, I began to see those same feet walk up to me that I saw in my dream at the age of four years old. Jesus took me by the hand and stood me up (while I was down on my face), and He cleaned all the debris off and breathed in me a newfound courage. Over and over, He repeated, "Do not doubt my creation! You are My creation! All that is in you is Me! Stop doubting who you are!" When I stood up from that encounter with Jesus, I realized something was different. It wasn't long before the revelation came: I WAS FREE FROM FEAR!! I suddenly knew what surrender meant. My chains were gone, and a journey of true transformation was beginning.

The next week during worship, I began to see what seemed to be like a movie clip of my pictures through my life. They started from my childhood, pictures of me riding my motorcycle, running through life with such a brave face. Then, the pictures began to get closer to my teen years and young adult years. One picture I always hated from the seventh grade was the picture that flashed before my eyes the most: a young, very fearful little girl. God zoomed the picture into my eyes, and all I could see was timidity. Then, suddenly, I saw myself standing before people, on what appeared to be a stage, arms bravely stretched into the air, my face that of a roaring lion. I didn't want it to end because I saw timidity gone and the strong, powerful, courageous person I feel inside standing there. I knew He was reminding me that I was free, and I would fulfill my call in freedom.

I thought I was going to be bound by fear forever, but the fears that bound me and kept me silent, the fears that bound me and kept me from taking steps of faith in my life, the fears that crippled me and bound me to the past, the fears that paralyzed me and made my call look impossible... He broke them off of me and as He has walked side by side with me through the healing process, I have been able to move forward in a newfound freedom that I have never known. It has been a process of ups and downs and a process of reminding myself, "I AM FREE!" every time I step in front of people. When God sets you free, you cannot allow the enemy to bring the bondage back. You just remind him that greater is He that is in you than he that is in the world, and if GOD is for you, who cares who is against you?

"It is for freedom that Christ has set us free. Stand firm, then, and do not let yourselves be burdened again by a yoke of bondage."

(Galatians 5:1 NIV)

Chapter 11
Re-defining A Fearless Identity

From 2015 to the present, God has continued me on a process of being re-defined. He has brought me to a place of knowing who I am in Him and who He is in me. He has pressed me, the Holy Spirit has searched me, and He has stretched me. The process God has taken me through has been that of a "pressing." That is the best way I can explain it. Even though the chains were shattered, I still needed to be re-defined. In the pressing over the last several years, God has removed old character traits that were built through the lens of fear and taught me what it means to walk in the character of Jesus Christ. He has removed old habits that weren't healthy for me and helped me build new habits that have matured me and taught me how to keep my focus on the call, not on the things around me. He has transformed my heart toward people, and we've cultivated a love together that allows me to love others unconditionally, the same way He loves you and me. He has taught me what it means to stay in a posture of surrender daily in order to build a relationship with Him that I have never had before.

Because I have chosen to surrender myself fully to Him, I now know who I am in Him and who He is in me.

Psalm 139:13 tells us that He formed our inward parts; He knitted us together in the womb of our mother. Genesis 1:26 tells us that God created us in HIS image (*tselem*: His resemblance, His shadow) and after His likeness (*demuwth*: manner, similar to Him). His image is love, authority, power, and kingship. His likeness is love, joy, peace, kindness, goodness, self-control, gentleness, patience, and faithfulness. He created us to be just like Him. So, what I finally had to ask myself was this: Why am I choosing to allow the enemy to tell me I am anything less than God's image? You and I are created in the image of our Father, the Alpha and Omega, the God that always has been and always will be, the God that loves us so much that He allowed His only son to die on a cross for us. This is the God in whose image we are created. We must stop allowing the enemy to whisper in our ears as he did with Eve.

I do not believe I have fully arrived at absolute perfection because we will be spending the rest of our lives on this earth being perfected by the Holy Spirit. However, the goal in our walk with God is to never get stagnant or go backwards. We should always be moving forward. Joshua 1:9 says, "Have I not commanded you? Be strong and courageous. Do not be afraid and do not be dismayed, for the LORD YOUR GOD is with you wherever you go."

We can only become strong and courageous when we finally allow God to have it all, to have our fears, our anger, our hurts, our past, our unforgiveness and our bitterness. We have to humble ourselves and lay pride down at His feet. We have to study and grasp the understanding of what it means to be carriers of the character, the presence, the glory of God. That is what I am allowing God to do in me for the rest of my life. I want Him to keep pressing me, searching me, and stretching me so that I am always growing spiritually and transforming culture everywhere I go.

Chapter 12
The Pressing, A Soul Cleanse

I want to take the next few pages to explain to you what I mean when I say I want Him to keep pressing me, searching me, and stretching me. As I described earlier, over the last several years I have been pressed down to nothing, searched into the deepest inner parts of me, and stretched beyond what I ever imagined I could. My desire is that my heartbeat literally beats with the pulse of God. I want to know Him so intimately that I act like Him—I carry His character, transform culture, and bring people into a life of restoration and reconciliation THROUGH HIS LOVE! We are told in 1 John 4:8 that he who does not love does not know God, for God is love. Let me tell you this: I want to know God at a level of deepness that none have ever fathomed. That means that I have to love others with the same love with which He loves me. This takes some pressing.

Have you ever heard the song, "When You Walk Into The Room" by Bryan and Katie Torwalt? That song absolutely rocks me every time I hear it. Why? Because WE carry the presence of Jesus Christ in us; we are carriers of the Kingdom of God, and when we walk into the room, atmospheres should shift, sickness should vanish, the spiritually dead begin to rise, and in us is the resurrection life. It's time we identify who we are and walk in it. THAT IS KINGDOM.

God created each of us with a desire for intimacy with Him, an intimacy that no earthly relationship can fill. It's an intimacy without which we are void of joy, peace, love, self-control, kindness, patience, faithfulness, goodness, and gentleness. We are void of His character, and without His character, we cannot follow through with our mandate, His purpose for every life He created on this earth: TO GO AND DISCIPLE THE NATIONS, TO GO AND CHANGE THE CULTURE AROUND US, TO BE CARRIERS OF HIM EVERYWHERE WE GO (Matthew 28:19). When we have fear in our root system, we keep God and anyone else an arm's length away. As you have learned through the story of my life, many things can be rooted in our soul, and these roots can be very beneficial or very destructive. My prayer is that the destructive roots are exposed and removed from your life as you finish this book. Many times, these roots are exposed through a process I call "the pressing." This is what it feels like, at least. In order to get to the purest form of oil from an olive, it has to be hard pressed, but the outcome is for our benefit. When God is pressing all of the impurities out of our lives, it is for our benefit and the benefit of the kingdom.

We are a three-part being just as God is a three-part being. We are spirit, soul, and body. When we come to the place of realizing the truth of who Jesus Christ is, truly believing in Him and confessing that belief, we become saved, (from the word *sozo*, which means to be whole, healed, delivered, preserved, protected). This is where your spirit man or the sin nature with which you were born becomes the spirit of Jesus Christ. He is now living in you. Your spirit man has become new, whole, healed, delivered, preserved, and protected.

"Because, if you confess with your mouth that Jesus is Lord and believe in your heart that God raised Him from the dead, you will be saved. For with the heart one believes and is justified, and with the mouth one confesses and is saved." Romans 10:9-10 (NKJV)

You still have to walk through soul salvation, and this is where so many in the body of Christ get stuck. I have heard it said so many times that once you pray the sinner's prayer, you are saved, and you become a new creation in Christ. Old things are passed away, and now, all things have become new. Yet, they do not realize this is talking about our spirit man, and we have a soul that will continue to struggle because it has a lot of roots planted deep within.

In Luke 19:9-10 (NKJV), Jesus says to Zacchaeus, "Today salvation has come to this house [habitation, dwelling place],... For the Son of man came to seek [desire] and to save [*sozo*] that which was lost [those separated into destruction]" (original language placed in the text). "Salvation" is the word *soteria*, which means "delivered, rescued, saved," and its foundational root word is *sozo*. Jesus came to this earth not to get billions of people to say a prayer of salvation; instead, He came to this earth desiring to show people what it means to be saved and gave us a blueprint in order to walk out the process of our salvation, so we are no longer separated into destruction, but instead set apart into Him!

The pressing starts when we come to that place of full surrender.

Many times, when God is taking us through the pressing process, we will find ourselves in a quiet, hidden place. Why would we find ourselves hidden? I believe it is because the pressing can become painful, ugly, and, yes, even scary. God never wants to expose us with our impurities to the world around us. He wants to take us to His secret place and do a good work; then, when we are ready, He will present us as His prized possession and place us exactly where we belong in order to walk out His purpose on this earth. We have the option to go to that quiet place and let Him privately work on those impurities or be exposed publicly; we choose—humility or pride.

The problem comes when we are neither listening nor being completely obedient. Partial obedience to His leading can bring as much destruction as complete disobedience. This is what happened to me. I chose partial obedience instead of full obedience because of the fear of man. This choice not only hurt myself, but I hurt many over whom I had influence. This caused me to take a major step back and realize that I had some impurities; I could let them be exposed to the world and continue a path of destruction, or I could submit in full obedience to God and let Him deal with these impurities in the secret place. I finally chose full surrender in the secret place. I believe with all my heart this is where the stripping began.

Before an olive can be cleaned, ground, and pressed, it has to be stripped from the tree. This is when you are hand-picked to be taken to the press. I look at this as God removing all the things in your life that do not belong, so He can work on the inside.

Let me tell you this: my partial disobedience wasn't me choosing a sinful lifestyle over what God ordained me to do. It was me choosing to attempt to not offend people in fear of not being accepted. You see, I love to serve and do. Honestly, though, there are times in our serving and doing that it becomes more about serving man than serving God. I love to serve, but at that time in my life, it was because I needed the approval of those around me. I was doing for God, but I was loving the praise of man. God ALWAYS knows better than we do, and He knew that where He is taking me, this mentality that came with a life of fears had to be stripped off of my life.

I was serving on the worship team, leading the women's ministry, helping teach different classes, and serving in a ministry which was a prophetic teaching team. I was also working a full-time job as a nurse, being a mom, being a wife, and trying to care for all those in my life. I was burying myself in works and believe me, this isn't the first time I have fallen into this trap. This time, though, I had to truly see it and wipe out this addiction for good. Slowly, God began stripping things from my life. He started with changing different things in our church. It was kind of unnerving, but it was all God. The small Sunday morning transition moment that was taken care of by the prophetic teaching team was removed to help the service transitions flow better, and then a few weeks later, the classes I was helping teach ended.

In the spring and summer of 2017, life in general became pretty busy, and I was struggling with the balancing act of all the duties into which I had put myself. I found myself too busy to prepare for the women's ministry, so I began bringing other speakers in to teach. I didn't mind this at all because I was still in that place of carrying the paralyzing fear of teaching a group of people. As this transpired, I began to get very discouraged. I had lost several platforms, and I was feeling pretty insignificant. My identity was found in my works, not in my Father.

In this same time frame, Abraham and I were also leaders of a life group in our church. We had led this group for over 3 years, and we absolutely loved and still do love all of those we led. But a year before, God had already been telling me it was time to pass the baton and hand off the life group. I was so scared to disappoint our group family that I refused. As I've mentioned before, I still carried that need for acceptance. We had chosen to take a break from the life group for the summer, and during that break, we decided to pass the leadership over to an amazing couple who we knew would run forward with it. Unfortunately, due to some circumstances that I am not at liberty to share, after this passing of the baton, we ended up losing not only our life group but numerous friendships. This was a very dark season for my family. My fear of man and the need for acceptance brought me to a place of pure brokenness.

There came a time in which God asked us to separate ourselves from everything taking place, and the downward spiral began, bringing a lot of hurt and bitterness to my heart. I didn't understand God's direction, and the more time that went by, the more bitter I became; my bitterness was not toward God but toward the actions of others in our lives, actions I just couldn't understand. I look back now and realize their actions toward us were because they didn't understand why God would tell us to separate, and it became about abandonment once again. Fear of abandonment is a paralyzing fear. It will keep you in a place of loneliness that no one should ever have to experience.

When you're seeking God and asking Him to move in your life, I promise you, He will strip you to spiritual nakedness.

A few months later, there was a major transition in our worship ministry, and many of us had to take a step back in order to allow the team to become stronger. I was not yet healed from what had been stirring in me from the months before when this happened. I was HURT! Once again, fear tried to move back in. I began to feel inadequate, as, apparently, I wasn't good enough for the team. I felt abandoned by people I highly respected and bent over backwards to serve; I felt angry because they took from me the one thing in which God had begun to absolutely transform me, and I was becoming so comfortable leading. I felt broken because I had to watch those I once served with do what my heart desired. I felt myself falling into a pit of despair. I can't explain how hard it was to pull out of the pit. I had lost every platform I had been given, or should I say now, maybe they were platforms I had taken for myself? I did not understand the "why" in all of this. I began to have anxiety attacks in my sleep that would wake me up because I couldn't breathe. I was having nightmares where I would wake up crying like a baby. I didn't want to go to church until after worship was over. It hurt me so deeply to walk in and not be a part of that team.

I was losing hope pretty rapidly. Why? Because everything was being stripped from me. I was so consumed with serving and doing that I wasn't being consumed with my Father's desires for me. He needed me on my knees in humility so that He could get my attention. I learned in this season that the only one I can truly trust is Him, the only one I need the approval of is Him, and at times, He has to remove people and things to teach us that. I also learned that my works mentality was part of the residue of living a life under the power of the fear of man. God desires truly humble vessels to do His kingdom work on this earth.

If you can't stay humble, you can't carry His power and authority and walk in dominion.

Chapter 13
Search My Heart, Oh God!

Then came the time of Him searching my innermost being. He took me through a serious season of being searched. He began revealing attitudes, hurts, pride, the things that were keeping me from being advanced to the next level. I felt like I was in one of those sci-fi movies where they shrink down the little spaceship and send someone into a person's body to find some hidden mystery. I felt like every time I got on my face before God, He and I would go on an adventure within myself, and He would reveal those things that needed to be removed. Some of those things were deeply embedded in me. Psalm 139:23-24 became my heart's cry: "Search me, God, and know my heart; test me and know my anxious thoughts. See if there is any offensive way in me and lead me in the way everlasting." Pray this prayer, and I promise you, life will begin to change.

How does the Holy Spirit search you? Through the study of God's Word! As you begin to study His Word, the Holy Spirit begins to search your inner depths, and He will begin to reveal your heart stance and true thoughts. Holding ourselves up to the mirror of the Word of God is how we are transformed. The more you seek Him, the more you begin to look like Him. Watch yourself transform from glory to glory, as 2 Corinthians 3:18 describes: "We all, with unveiled face, beholding as in a mirror the glory of the Lord, are being transformed into the same image from glory to glory, just as by the Spirit of the Lord."

God began to reveal to me that I served for approval. I was so busy doing that I wasn't focusing on simply being. I loved the platform because it made me feel important, and the only way to show me that was to take it away. Let me tell you, I went through a period of true grieving. You may think that sounds weird, but when something you deeply love is taken away, it hurts, especially when you believe in your heart you're doing it for God. I firmly believe much of the grieving that took place was just the revelation of why I was doing what I was doing. When I realized I was doing this out of bad character that was attached to that past fear, I was crushed because once again, I felt like I had disappointed God.

He also began to reveal to me that I had a lot of pride and unforgiveness built up. As I've mentioned before, my family has walked through a lot of betrayal and hurt over the last fifteen years, and although I felt like I had forgiven, I had not. I remember so many times I would say, "I have forgiven," only to hear a name or see a picture and feel the anger immediately rise up. God showed me so many ways that I was wrong. In fact, He revealed to me that the anxiety attacks I was having in my sleep resulted from deep-rooted unforgiveness toward others that had been planted throughout my lifetime. As He began searching and revealing to me the things that were hidden and needed to go, a transition began to happen inside of me.

One of the roots He revealed through the searching process was one about which I had no clue. I am a person of honor, loyalty, and integrity. It's just who I am because of God in me. As God has broken the pride, I've kept these scriptures before me daily: Isaiah 57:15 (NKJV), "I dwell in the high and holy place with him who has a contrite and humble spirit, to revive the spirit of the humble and to revive the heart of the contrite ones," and Isaiah 66:2 (NIV), "The Lord says, 'These are the ones I look on with favor: those who are humble and of a contrite spirit, and who trembles at My word.'" God dwells with those who have a reverential fear of him and who walk in a contrite and humble spirit. Pride and the spirit of God cannot dwell in the same habitation.

The root was this fear of rejection from leadership. I honored them with all that was in me, but I was always afraid to speak what was in my heart. I would sit in meetings with my heart pounding out of my chest, which is usually what happens when God has given me a prophetic word to speak, but I couldn't let it out. I began to tell my husband that I did not feel I had a voice. With everything else that had been stripped away, I felt like that had been, too. After months of this struggle, I went into my Senior Leaders' office, sat them down, and began to share with them my feelings. Pastor Marquieta saw the root and was able to expose it, and because of that, I was able to uproot it right then and there. It was a root that had been placed by past leadership that did not really allow me to have a voice; even when I did speak, it was never heard. Because of that, I believed even if I spoke, I would not be heard. This was so freeing for me. I wonder today if they wish at times they had just left that little root there because I'm sure I talk a little too much now.

The more I let go of those roots, the more I began to look in that spiritual mirror and see my Father instead of ugliness and fear. Am I there yet? Absolutely not! But I've come a long way, baby! I stay on my knees daily, keeping myself in check with the truths of His Word, making sure I stay in a posture of humility and love.

Chapter 14
Stretching Is Painful

Any time God begins to move in our lives, we will walk through different steps. We've talked about the pressing, the stripping, the searching and now... the stretching. He began to stretch me in ways that I have never been stretched!

As Holy Spirit began to speak to me about forgiveness, bitterness, and anger, He showed me how I was being paralyzed in the spirit because I refused to let go and forgive those I held these offenses toward. The Word tells us that if we have unforgiveness or offense toward another, we aren't forgiven by God (Matthew 6:14-15, Mark 11:25). We are also told in Matthew 5:23-24 if we are going to the altar and remember that someone has something against us, we are to go and be reconciled then come back to the altar. God told me to go to these people and repent. This wasn't just for my spiritual health; it was for theirs also. Talk about a pride buster! God is good at breaking pride. God is a God of honor, and when we are walking in unforgiveness and offense, then we are dishonoring God. How? We are all His kids, and when we dishonor each other, we dishonor our Father. Never forget, pride is rooted in fear. If pride is being revealed, the best question to ask God is, "To what fear is this connected?"

Break the fear! Break the cycle!

Another way He stretches us is by getting us out of our comfort zones and making us face fear. I told you earlier, I LOVE TO SING. It's a God-given gift, but I know my anointing is to teach. I hid from my teaching by staying on the worship team, so God removed it! He will do that if we aren't listening. I wasn't comfortable teaching, but I had such a desire to do so.

In January of 2018, we started a teaching team and began the process of breaking down the book of John verse by verse. We began teaching it on Wednesday nights, and God used the book of John to fully heal me and bring me to a place of restoration and to a whole new level of teaching. He is such an amazing God!

He stretched me by putting me in positions that I personally would not choose because of my history of fearing man's thoughts. He began to prove to me that He is the one that called me, not man! We have a promise in His Word that says, "The kingdom of God is not a matter of eating and drinking, but of righteousness, peace, and joy in the Holy Spirit. For he who serves Christ in these things is accepted by God and approved by men" (Romans 14:17-18). When we are truly serving God with a kingdom mindset of righteousness, peace, and joy, we do not have to worry about proving anything to man. We are automatically accepted by God, and in that acceptance, He gives us the favor and approval of men.

Don't let the fear of man keep you from walking with the Kingdom in mind.

He began to stretch me by putting people in my life that I normally would not go to for a friendship. He knows who we need in our lives way more than we do, and those people are called connectors. One thing He taught me in the last twenty years is that He knows who belongs and who doesn't belong in our lives season after season. This is a very hard part of our spiritual walk to grasp. If you are anything like me, then you want to keep all of your friends close forever. But not every relationship is here for a lifetime, and we have to be okay with that in order to keep moving forward.

This makes me think of Jesus. He had twelve pretty close friends and three within that circle that He was very close to: Peter, James, and John. These three probably thought Jesus would be by their side until they all grew old and died together. Jesus, however, had a purpose to fulfill, and not even His three closest friends could accompany Him. It wasn't a season that would last forever, but it was a season in which they had to stay while He went. If Jesus had to walk it, we know we will have to do so, too. The stripping and the stretching can pretty much go hand-in-hand at times.

Through the deep study of His Word, He began to transform me from the inside out. Pride had been revealed and broken, bitterness brought to the surface and removed, unforgiveness revealed and forgiveness given, any and all hardness in my heart removed, and a new level of God-love now fills my life. I look at myself today and do not know who I am. I see people in a totally different way, and I pray daily for my actions to mirror the image of my Father.

Let me now reiterate my sentiment from earlier: I want this to go into the depths of your soul. When we study His Word and the depths of what it truly means, there is no way to walk away unchanged. God is all about transformation. Again, He says in 2 Corinthians 3:18, "We all, with unveiled face, beholding as in a mirror the glory of the Lord, are being transformed into the same image from glory to glory, just as by the Spirit of the Lord." His Word brings a pressing that strips us of the old man, searches our innermost being in order to remove old behaviors, chains that bind, and anything holding us back, and then stretches us out of our comfort zones and old nature in order to set us on the journey called purpose.

Many times, we want self-help books or someone to just make it happen for us, but I am here to tell you, the only self-help manual is the Word of God, and the only person who can make it happen for us is the person of the Holy Spirit in us. I will never again let someone tell me that it is not possible to be fearless. I have been told that by people I looked up to, and I have heard it taught in sermons, but I promise you, through Jesus Christ, you can be fearless! Will fear attempt to bombard you? Absolutely, but you will be fearless and courageous enough to say, "Fear Cannot Have Me!" as you run straight at it.

Chapter 15
It's His Perfect Love

I truly believe the only way we will walk free from fear is to know His perfect love. The reason for this is because we are told in 1 John 4:18 (NKJV) that "there is no fear in love; but perfect love casts out fear, because fear involves torment. He who fears has not been made perfect in love."

Although I was set free from the bondage of fear in 2015, I continued to walk in what I call the residue left over from all the years of believing fear. The torment of fear will leave some sticky, gross residue behind. In November 2018, God took me into the secret place for over three months and began to teach me of the depths of His love. I had been telling Him in my short little prayer times that I wanted the fullness of the freedom from all the leftover residue of my negative life experiences. I honestly had no clue what I was asking. I had spent a few years waking up by 6 am and heading straight to the gym for cross-fit, then back home to get ready for my day. My prayer time happened in the few minutes of my shower before I would turn on a preaching message from YouTube and listen as I got ready for the day. This wasn't enough for my Father, and I was to soon discover this. He asked me to stop going to the gym first thing in the morning, He said He wanted my mornings. That was a huge sacrifice for me, but I was so ready for that final step of freedom that I would do anything at that point. So, I stopped. I continued getting up at the same time, but I steered my tired self straight to my prayer room and began to spend the first few hours of my day hidden away, just me and my Father. It was life transforming.

At the time of writing this book, I have continued this on a daily basis. When you are obedient to God, change is inevitable. Nothing can stop it because you are allowing Him into those deep places. He began to speak to me about His love. I mean, I thought I knew His love, but I was so wrong. Remember me telling you that we can get so caught up doing that we forget about being? Yes, we can do the same thing with His love. He took me to Revelations 2:2-4: "I know your works, your labor, your patience, and that you cannot bear those who are evil. You have tested those who say they are apostles and are not, and have found them liars; and you have persevered and have patience, and have labored for My name's sake and have not become weary. Nevertheless... I have this against you, that you have left your first love!"

My heart felt like it stopped beating for a moment. I repented to my Father for being so busy with life in general that I had forgotten to put Him first. I began to realize that although I wanted true freedom, I apparently wanted other things more-- things like a good workout, a cup of coffee with a friend, getting to the office to start my day, or just sleeping in and taking my time getting ready. Is there anything wrong with any of this? Absolutely not! But for me, I put all of these things before my heavenly Father, and He must only be first in our lives.

As I continued through the three months of studying His love, I just began to melt on the inside. My heart posture changed, my attitude towards others changed, and I began to have this righteous anger rise up inside of me because I want all of the church to see the truth of who He is and know His love for them. I began to have this anger because I began to see how wrong we, as the church body, were acting. The love of God has become a distant thing in the church as a whole. There's gossip taking place daily, even in the church during church services, and there are so-called Christians bashing other Christians on social media constantly. We have churches accepting things that are absolute abominations to God, and He tells us so in His word. We've stopped teaching Truth because of the fear of not having a large enough crowd inside of our building, I mean, heaven forbid anyone get offended by the Holy Spirit and actually change their lives. This, my friends, is what I began to see, and my heart began to break. But as long as I was walking in the residue of all the fears of my own life and not fully encapsulated in His love, I couldn't see all of it. To be honest, I was probably part of some of it.

When God asks us to take a step of obedience, it's always going to be because He wants to bring a form of transformation in our lives. He wants to bring us to another level, a deeper level in Him. 1 Corinthians 13:13 (NKJV) tells us to abide in "faith, hope, and love, but the greatest of these is love." When we are abiding in love, we are abiding in God because God is love. When we are abiding in Him, then we begin to bear the fruit of His character in our lives, and this brings internal transformation that not only works in you, but through you. Abiding in Him reveals His character to us. 1 Peter 1:5 tells us He who called us is Holy, so we are to be holy in all of our conduct (all of our being), because it is written, "be holy for I AM HOLY." God is holy, and God is love, so we cannot walk a life of love without a life of holiness and vice versa. His character is both, and in both of those, there is life-transforming power.

This was the final touch to my freedom from fear and all it had built in my belief system. My life, my family, my faith, the ministry, the messages, the prophetic, the love for other people has not and will not ever be the same. I discovered the victory over fear through the knowledge of the Word of God and His love for me, and you can, too!

Romans 8:38-39 (ESV): "For I am sure that neither death nor life, nor angels nor rulers, nor things present nor things to come, nor powers, nor height nor depth, nor anything else in all creation, will be able to separate us from the love of God in Christ Jesus our Lord."

Chapter 16
Fear Cannot Have Me

As I sit here today writing this book, my mind is blown away at all God has done as I have surrendered. I look back and realize that in every single event of my life, He was setting the stage for my purpose. Fifteen years ago, I was hiding from the public eye; ten years ago, I was attempting to make it work but failing at every turn; and five years ago, I was moving forward $1/16^{th}$ of an inch at a time because fear was so gripping, but my strong will kept pushing. Today, I am traveling and speaking into men and women in other regions and states, as I continue to envision transformation for the nations. I am leading a phenomenal women's ministry and watching God transform their lives right before me. My husband and I are part of the apostolic governance of our church, teaching and leading the pastoral arm of the ministry. I am leading groups of teachers, and we are able to give voice to our hearts and desires because we aren't fearful of each other's thoughts. He is using my voice, which fear once kept silent, to break the chains of bondage and set the captives free. He has set me free from the fear of man and replaced it with a love and desire for their growth because when you are free from the fear of man, you can preach and teach like most can't. Why? Because you aren't afraid of offending them. Jesus Christ was not afraid of offending anyone; in fact, He offended religious rulers all the time.

Yes, I promise, I do speak through the filters of grace and love, but I will not speak anything but biblical truth. There is no other way. God has placed a mandate on my life to break the bondage of the religious mindset holding people back from kingdom living. I will run my race with a fierce heart because fear can't have me! None of this is meant to be read as bragging on me. I am bragging on my God. He is the God in me, around me, and working through me. I would still be a bound-up ball of fearful chains if it wasn't for Him. It just takes an obedient vessel willing to say, "Yes God! Here I am, use me. I will run the race You set before me!"

The Word tells us in Hebrews 12:1, "Therefore, since we are surrounded by such a great cloud of witnesses, let us throw off everything that hinders and the sin that so easily entangles. And let us run with perseverance the race set before us!" God has a race for all of us to run, but when we are chained to the roots of our past, then we are simply running in place and digging a deep rut out of which we will struggle to get out of. God wants us to throw off everything—EVERYTHING--that is hindering us from our mandate on this earth. Letting go of the fear, anger, bitterness, unforgiveness, and even negative declarations we have spoken over ourselves or others have spoken over us is key in this spiritual season.

If you are reading this book, then I believe the enemy has attempted to paralyze you with his lies of fear also. Isaiah 60:1-2 says, "Arise, shine, for your light has come, the glory of the Lord is risen upon you. Darkness [lack of knowledge] covers the earth and thick darkness is over the peoples, but the Lord rises upon you and His glory appears over you." Fear has gripped you long enough! It is time for you to rise up in the knowledge of the Word, which will overcome the lies of darkness. His glory is here in this exact moment, and it is upon you to set you free. It is time for you to see yourself in Christ and walk in the identity of who He created you to be.

I am declaring freedom over every person who reads this book: freedom from all bondages and fears, and freedom from lies and the whispering voice of the enemy. He does not have a foothold in your life anymore.

John 8:32: "you shall know the Truth [the Word, Jesus Christ]), and the Truth will make you free!"

As you are transformed from a life of fear to a life of freedom in Christ, you will find yourself longing to know more about Him. You will find yourself in situations facing fear but with a newfound courage to run straight at it, showing fear who truly has the victory. This new life you will discover needs to be founded on holiness, purity, and perseverance. The next few pages are daily devotionals on which you can focus as you rediscover these foundational truths in your life of freedom.

Just as God spoke over Joshua, I speak over you:

"Be strong and courageous, for the Lord is with you

wherever you go!"

Section II:

Free from Fear and Rooted in Holiness

7-Day Devotional Study On The Letters Of Apostle Peter

Day 1: ⟶ *You Are Set Apart*

I have heard "A call to holiness" in my spirit, over and over to the point that it's so deep in my heart I can't seem to move on to any other subject. Before I began hearing this phrase, I had been in prayer asking God to let me see in this generation a glory fire like we've never seen before. As I continue to seek God, I keep hearing Him say, "I want to pour out MORE of Me, but my people aren't ready; their hearts aren't pure before Me! It's time for a call back to holiness. Those who have ears to hear will hear and heed the call." The "MORE" is His glory! It's the realm of Him many never tap into. Glory is Kabowd—the weighty presence of God, the manifested presence in the now. I began to read about Peter: how people were healed when they got close enough to him to get under his shadow and how he truly walked in the glory of God. Peter was fearless because of God's glory in his life.

There are so many references to God's glory from the beginning to the end of the Word. In Exodus, God led the children of Israel by way of His glory cloud by day and the glory fire by night. His glory protected them and confused the enemy's army. His glory sanctifies. Isaiah tells us we are created for His glory and that His glory will not be given over to idols. This made me ask myself, "What am I seeking over God?"

1 Chronicles tells us that we are to declare His glory. Psalms tells us over and over to declare His glory, and we are reminded that His glory is the manifestation of His Kingdom (Power, authority, Dominion).

Isaiah and Ezekiel tell us that His glory will be seen by ALL nations—that it is going to come like a rushing water over this earth and it will shine! In John, we are told that His glory manifests in miracles. We are also reminded in Romans that we are to SEEK His glory. Recently, I read a phrase in a book by Apostle Ryan LeStrange, and I grabbed a hold of it and made a determination to figure it out: *"When you enter the glory, you leave the limitations of the earth."* This is where we begin to see the power of God manifest in our lives through signs, miracles, and wonders. Who else is ready to start truly seeing the miracle working power of God in this region? In our homes? In our day-to-day lives?

I began asking God, "How did Peter and others on this earth discover the depths of your glory? How did they get so close to You that Your glory literally touched every life that came 'near' them? How did they tap into that realm of power and authority?" God told me if I was so curious, I should read 1st and 2nd Peter and study them in depth. I spent several weeks in quiet study, and God rocked every part of me through it.

I am going to be saying this a lot: **It's about walking in holiness**, living a life surrendered to God with a pure heart, and not allowing anyone or anything but Him on the throne of our life. It's about laying down the passions and desires of our flesh (our old, unsaved nature) and walking in the revelation of Jesus Christ.

1 Peter is all about our soul's salvation. Peter tells us numerous times throughout the whole book that we are to stay pure before God. In chapter 1, he tells us to prepare our minds for action (understanding and deep thought) and to be sober minded (discreet, watchful, awake and temperate- disciplined), not allowing intoxicating thoughts or influences to numb us and keep us from evaluating things correctly, so we see clearly! I want you to think about this for a moment: intoxicating thoughts or influences. Let's take just a second and remove "alcohol" from the picture. Yes, alcohol and drugs can cause intoxication (the loss of control of behavior, physical or mental control markedly diminished), and Peter does talk a lot about not being a drunk, but I want to take you a little deeper. He says keep a sober mind, and some versions say sober spirit. We allow so much into our mind that causes us to lose

control of our godly behavior and causes our mental and physical control to be diminished, making it difficult for the Holy Spirit to influence us. Think about this—fear, depression, oppression, unforgiveness, bitterness, anxiety, etc.—all of these numb us. They keep us from being able to spiritually see and hear clearly and from being spiritually awake, watchful, and disciplined. This is why I believe we are told in Phil. 4:8, "Whatever is true, just, pure, lovely, commendable, worthy of respect, excellent or praiseworthy, think on these things!" God wants our thoughts on HIM. He wants us disciplined in all areas...He wants us living a holy life!

    He goes on to mention that Grace will only be brought to us through the revelation of Jesus Christ. Guys, this is big! I am so tired of hearing this "grace" message that people use in order to live a life of "freedom" to do **as they please** because grace covers them. Much of the church has truly lost the understanding of holiness and the fear of the Lord. Peter tells us here that grace is only brought to us at the revelation of Jesus Christ in our lives. In other words, when we truly grasp who Jesus is IN our lives, we will no longer desire to live a sinful lifestyle. Will we mess up? YES! But because we know who we are IN HIM, we will be quick to repent, and His grace will redeem, cover, and restore us. When we don't truly have a revelation of Jesus Christ and what He did for us, then a sinful life is no big deal, and I dare say His grace is lifted until we truly choose to repent and follow Him. Grace isn't permission to live an unholy lifestyle yet claim to be righteous! When we have the revelation of Jesus Christ in our lives, we are no longer ignorant. We now know the choice of holy conduct vs unholy conduct is ours.

He also tells us in 1 Peter 1 that we are called to holiness. We are not redeemed with corruptible things, but we were ransomed with the blood of Jesus Christ, His precious blood. Why on earth do we choose unholy conduct? We are called to walk in a pure heart and pure love before our God. Peter reminds us that we purify our souls (mind/will/emotions) and walk with a pure heart by obeying the truth through the Holy Spirit and loving others—because God is love. I want to encourage you to get your Word out and read 1 and 2 Peter!

I truly believe God is calling us back to a lifestyle of holy conduct, but there is only a specific remnant of people who are going to heed his call. I personally choose to be one. Living a holy life means much sacrifice. Sometimes, your family isn't going to understand the choices the Holy Spirit asks you to make, and sometimes we won't even understand, but we have to trust that God knows best and rest in that reassurance. When we truly put our trust in God, in all honesty, there's no need for human understanding. We just have to be willing and obedient.

Father, I surrender myself to you today! I surrender my fleshly desires to run my own life. I surrender it all to You! Father, I know that even though I personally may not understand, I choose to walk pure, holy, and humble before You. I lay down my own will, my own dreams, my own wants, and say YES to Your will and dreams for me! Holy Spirit, go into the depths of my soul and reveal to me the things that keep me walking in an unclean, unholy, impure life so that I can, in turn, repent and be cleansed and covered by Your blood and Your grace. I want to be a part of the remnant you are calling to walk in Your glory. I am a glory carrier! In Jesus' name, Amen!

Personal Notes:

Day 2: ⟶ *Stay Humble*

At the end of 1 Peter 1, Peter is telling us that the Word of God endures forever, but flesh and the glory of man withers away like the grass. Then he goes on to say "THEREFORE…" Remember, we should always look back to see why the writer uses "therefore" because they are connecting it to what they said previously. He is explaining that because we are now living with souls purified before God, it's time to lay aside the flesh. YUCK! That's the part none of us really want to hear. In other words, get that soulish realm in check with the Holy Spirit and start walking in self-control.

He says, "Lay aside all ill-will and bad nature, all craftiness and deceit, all hypocrisy – acting as someone you are not and dissimulation, all corruptness and jealousy, all evil speaking – back biting, slander, talk against others, gossip as the immature (newborns) in Christ would do but desire and long for the Word of God as a child desires to learn, growing into your salvation." Matthew 18:3 even reminds us that unless you become as a little child (having that desire and willingness to learn, grow, and love), you will not inherit the Kingdom of God. In other words, as long as you walk around with a "know it all" attitude, living in the flesh, not learning or growing in Christ and being prideful, you will NOT walk in the authority, power, and LOVE of the Kingdom. You will not experience all the Kingdom of God is on earth as it is in heaven.

Did you know that God has chosen us as living stones? Jesus Christ was a carpenter, but one thing I want you to remember is that in His days, everything was built out of stone, and just as cement is now our way of making solid foundations before building a home, stone was theirs. In Isaiah 28:16, the Lord says, "Behold, I lay in Zion a stone for a foundation, a tried stone, a precious cornerstone, a sure foundation; WHOEVER believes will not act hastily." This is a prophecy about Jesus Christ. He is the chief cornerstone, the strength, the foundation all the rest of God's living stones are built upon! Peter goes on to say that HE, God, is building us up into spiritual houses, a holy priesthood through Jesus Christ. But first, we have to believe this, and in that believing, He comes in and begins such an amazing work. The word tells us that honor is for those who believe but stumbling and offense are for those who choose not to believe.

Those who believe in Jesus Christ and are living a life of surrender to Him, those who have confessed with their mouths and placed Him on the throne of their hearts ARE A CHOSEN GENERATION, a royal priesthood, a HOLY PEOPLE – His OWN special people. That is so amazing! He chose us, and He calls us HIS OWN. He reached down into the darkest parts of our life and pulled us out into the glorious truth of His light. In His mercy, He SAVED US! Why would we not want to walk holy before Him? How can we not want to fall on our face in worship before the one who literally died to cover our sin?

So many times, this is because we are still waring with the desires of our flesh, our soulish realm. Peter goes on in verse 11 to say, "Beloved, I BEG you, abstain from fleshly [carnal – worldly] lusts which war against the soul." When we give in to the flesh (walk in worldly conduct), it does two things. First, it keeps us from spiritually maturing; this is soul salvation which we will forever be walking out because we are all born with a fleshly nature, but it's so important to allow Holy Spirit in to guide us DAILY. Second, it gives the world something to hold over our heads AND keeps them from wanting God. The world is looking for hypocrites – they will find anything they can to say, "Oh, you call yourself a Christian?" and they will point their fingers at us and say, "That's why I don't go to church. It's just full of fake people."

Peter tells us not to give anyone reason to speak evil against us but to only give them reason to glorify God. Honorable conduct, my friend, is living a holy lifestyle. Peter goes on to say that by living free and in holy conduct, honoring EVERYONE, loving our fellow man, fearing God and honoring ALL leadership (governmental, too 😉) that we silence the foolish and ignorant. They won't have a reason to point a finger. In verse 21, Peter says for this WE WERE

CALLED. Christ suffered for us, leaving us an example that we should follow:

- He did not walk in sinful nature.
- He spoke no deceit.
- When reviled (reproached and abused), He did not return it.
- When suffering, He did not threaten.
- He trusted Himself to God.

Jesus took on our sins in His own body so that WE could live in righteousness (right standing with God), walking in healing and restoration, knowing that He is the shepherd and overseer (guardian) of our souls.

Jesus Christ is Kingdom character! He came to this earth as an example of holy conduct and living. He has called each of us to be a part of His royal priesthood and holy nation, but we must return to the reverence of God that drops us to our knees, and we must return to a holy lifestyle that keeps us pure before Him. Is it a journey? ABSOLUTELY! Peter even said, "I beg you as sojourners and pilgrims, abstain from fleshly lusts." In other words, we are on a journey, and we are going to make mistakes; we are all going to step away from holiness more than we truly want, or at least think we have, but the amazing thing is that God truly is a God of grace, and He truly does forgive us, pick us up, dust us off and set us back on our path; HOWEVER, we have to be humble enough to admit and allow it. Pride keeps us from so much and keeps us constantly in the flesh. As I Peter 5:6 says, "Humble yourselves, therefore, under the mighty hand of God so that at the proper time He may exalt you!" Keeping ourselves humble keeps our hearts pure because we stay open and honest before God, and we receive correction and direction.

Father, all I can say is help me to keep a contrite and humble spirit and attitude before You. Your Word says in Isaiah 66:2 THIS is the one to whom YOU look: he who is humble and contrite in spirit and trembles at Your Word. I desire Your Word, and I ask that You give me a newfound reverence for You and Your Word. Father, I want to walk holy, pure, and humble before You. Thank You for loving me, being so very patient with me, and for showering me with grace and mercy as I continue to journey with You. I am Yours, and You are mine. Holy Spirit help me to walk with a humble heart and in the love of God toward all those in my life. Break all pride off of me. In Jesus' name, Amen.

Personal Notes:

*Day 3: ⟶ **Stay Aligned***

At the end of chapter 2, Peter talks about Jesus, our ultimate example. He explains His conduct and how He took on all our sins so that we could walk in righteousness and healing. Because of what Jesus did on that cross, we can now return to Him, the Shepherd and Guardian/Overseer of our lives.

Then, he begins chapter 3 by calling all believers to humility, holiness, submission, and service. He says in the same way that Jesus conducted himself, WE are also to do so. He speaks to wives in verses 1-2: "In the same way [as Jesus would], you should patiently accept the authority of your husbands." This is so that even if they do not obey God's Word, as they observe your pure, respectful conduct, they may be persuaded WITHOUT A WORD by THE WAY YOU LIVE.

I absolutely love this because when I look at this, I don't just see it as husbands and wives; I see it as with anyone God places in our lives as an authority figure, and yes, sometimes that authority will be a woman. Many religious and non-Christian circles have used these few verses to beat women into ungodly submission. Seriously, I have seen it many times within many close relationships throughout my life. Being a woman who preaches and teaches to both men and women I, myself, have been persecuted by many, misled family and religious circles included. But this is not Peter's point. Peter is not telling women that they are under the man, that they are to submit at every command even to the point of abuse, and they are never to lead. He is telling us that we are to conduct ourselves as Jesus did. Jesus understood his umbrella of authority – God covered Him, and He was fully submitted to the will of God. Yet, God allowed Him to make His own choices. Submission, from the Greek *hypotasso* (hypo – by, with, in, among, under) (tasso – arrange, ordain, set, appoint = position), is a Greek military term meaning "to arrange [troop divisions] in a military fashion under the command of a leader." In non-military use, it was "a voluntary attitude of giving in, cooperating, assuming responsibility, and carrying a burden." To walk in submission, be it to husband, leadership, government, boss, whoever is your authority figure at the time, is to voluntarily give of self as you assist in assuming responsibility and helping to carry the burden. It is a cooperation of people, not a control and rule from one person.

In other words, Peter is telling us that we are to walk just as Jesus walked, loving others, cooperating, and working side by side, allowing those to lead us as God leads them, and when we are walking out our life with this conduct, respecting even those who aren't respecting us, loving even those who aren't loving us back, we will win them to Christ simply by what they see, not what we preach at them. They will be persuaded WITHOUT A WORD by THE WAY YOU LIVE.

Peter goes on to explain that the beauty we should seek is not just outward appearance only, but that we should constantly have Him on the throne of our hearts. Our inner beauty should reflect outwardly. How? By carrying an incorruptible quality: I see this as not allowing all the things that Peter talks about in chapters 1 and 2 to affect us (See last 2 devotionals); by walking in humility and meekness with a peaceable spirit.

Let me tell you this: NONE of this is possible if we are not fully, intimately connected to Christ. This is all His character; this is all Kingdom mindedness. This is why we have so many in the body of Christ running people away from God instead of drawing them closer, because most in the body are not truly connected in intimacy with Christ. The Word tells us in James 4:8, "Draw near to God and He will draw near to you. Cleanse your hands and make your hearts pure, stop being double minded!" and in John 12:32, we read, "When I am lifted up from the earth, I will draw all people to myself!" When we believe in Jesus Christ, He makes His home inside of us. When we lift Him up by portraying His character, actions, and love to this world, people are drawn to the realness, the authenticity, and the love in you because He is drawing them to Him IN YOU. Oh, the lives that will be rocked when we start allowing Christ in us to show outwardly.

Peter goes on to tell the men to understand, respect, and value their wives as equal heirs in life and as we do respect, understand, and value each other, then we know nothing will get in the way of our prayers. Walking in humility, forgiveness, and love is vital if we want our prayers to be heard. Many verses in the Word tell us this. Peter stresses many times throughout his writings that we are to stay pure and humble before God to walk in holiness and honor.

He ends this chapter reminding us that, in order to love life and see good days, we must refrain from speaking deceit, negativity, subtlety, etc., and we must keep our thoughts aligned with the Word of God, avoiding the evil (bad nature). We must walk a life of reverential fear towards God and let go of the fear of man. Verse 13 says, "Who is he who will harm you if you become followers of what is good?" When the fear of man leaves your life, it brings about a whole new level of surrender to God, and you no longer fear full obedience to anything He asks of you. We should continuously acknowledge the holiness of God in our hearts and always be ready to stand up for our faith.

Father, this has been an interesting journey of learning to crucify the flesh, to lay aside all these fleshly emotions and truly surrender the throne of my heart to You. Holy Spirit continue to go into the depths of me and bring to light anything in me that is not of Christ's character so that I may be Him to all those I encounter. I know I will continue to make mistakes, and my mouth or feelings may get in the way at times, but I ask that You immediately bring my wrong actions to my attention and give me the strength to cast down anything that is not of You, God! Forgive me for allowing the flesh to take over in so many ways recently and purify my lips and humble my character once again. I love you, Father, and I fully surrender to the pressing and crushing it's going to take to bring out the new wine of Your Kingdom. In Jesus' name, Amen.

Personal Notes:

Day 4: ⟶ *Rejoice in Suffering*

The last part of 1 Peter 3 tells us of Christ's suffering once for our sins so that we may be brought to God through the same process of being put to death in the flesh (fleshly desires, worldly conduct, sinful nature) but made alive by the Spirit. Just as Christ suffered on this earth, he is letting us know that those who follow Him will suffer in one way or another.

When we think about suffering for Christ, a lot of times, we go back to the martyrs that have been put to death in some very gruesome ways, and some people will allow that to keep them from serving Him. But I want you to stop and think for a moment. To suffer for Christ may look like being condemned by those living in the world, being made fun of or misunderstood. It may look like loneliness because those who used to like the old, worldly person suddenly do not like the new person God is creating in you. It may also look like being disowned by family members who don't believe. It may be many different things, but one thing the Word promises us is this: it is better to suffer for God than it is to suffer in the world.

In 1 Peter 4, Peter is pretty much telling us that enough of our time has been spent living like the world and that it's time to arm ourselves with the mind of Jesus Christ and start living as He lived on this earth. I couldn't agree more! He was willing to suffer persecution in order to walk a holy life. This is the reason I have called this series "A Call to Holiness," because so much of the church has allowed so much of the world into their lives that we can't tell a difference anymore.

Please know that this has been as much for my knowledge as it has been for anyone else. As I mentioned in my previous devo, I was seeking God—asking Him to show me what I was doing wrong, what was keeping me from walking in the true holiness, the character and the love of Jesus Christ (that's our purpose, right? To bring the culture of heaven to this earth?), and what was keeping me from experiencing the manifestation of His Glory like Peter did. He sent me on this journey. He's shown me some of it was fear, some of it was people, and some of it was simply a lack of knowledge. Not all have understood my decisions and convictions, but I'm okay with that; those who God wants surrounding me will understand and grow along with me.

Peter informs us that ignorance (spiritual), lust (unbridled desires), drunkenness, gossip, reveling, carousing, and idolatry (allowing idols in our lives – these idols can be many, many things: status, people, material things, emotions, anything that takes the place of God in your life—anything that you seek first before seeking Him) are all the ways of the world and that none of this should be in those who truly understand the holiness of God and follow Him. When all of these things are removed from our lives, the world will look at us as strange. They will not understand your decision to not join in what they believe as fun. This is okay. To suffer for Christ is to gain.

I was reading in 1 John 2 recently, and he made it very clear in verses 15-17 that for those who love the ways of the world, the love of the Father is not in them. Those who abide in the Father will not walk in the lusts of the flesh (those things mentioned above), the lust of the eyes, and the pride of life. This has been a very hard pill for me to swallow as I have studied this out. The more I learn and ask God to guide me into His holiness, the more I realize in what I was caught up. Many times, this is innocent, especially for those who are new Christians following more seasoned Christians. If the more seasoned Christians are allowing this in their lives, they are more than likely going to lead the new Christians astray. If you find yourself in a dry, lifeless season, I dare you to take the time and ask God, "What have I allowed in my life that is keeping me from tapping into the fullness of You?" He will reveal it.

One of my favorite parts of chapter 4 is towards the end when he says, "do not think it strange concerning the fiery trial which is to try you… but rejoice that you partake of Christ's sufferings because WHEN HIS GLORY IS REVEALED you may also be glad with exceeding joy! Those who have been reproached for Christ have the Spirit of GLORY and of GOD resting upon them." He reminds us not to be ashamed when suffering for Christ, but do not let yourself get caught up suffering as a murderer (1 John 3:15 – to hate a brother is the same as murder), a thief, or a busybody in other people's matters. It's time to learn what it means to truly abide in Him. 1 John 3 informs us that for those who ABIDE in Him, there is no habitual sin, and those who ABIDE in Him love each other in deed and in truth.

Going back a few verses in 1 Peter 4, he tells us, "Above all things have fervent love for one another, for love will cover a multitude of sins." How on earth does love cover a multitude of sins? I believe it's because those walking in love, just as John tells us, cannot desire a sinful life, and it covers, protects, and keeps us from entering into that sinful behavior. Ultimately, sin is not believing who you are in Christ; it is doubting the truths that God has given you. Look at Eve: the sin wasn't eating the fruit; it was questioning who God already said she was. He said they were created in His image, but the serpent made her question her identity. He said, "God knows that in the day you eat of the tree your eyes will be opened, and you will be like God, knowing good and evil." The result of her disbelief was sin behavior. When we are walking in His love, abiding in His love, and allowing Him to revolutionize us from the inside out through His holiness and glory, we get a knowing in our spirit. We know who and whose we are, and the desire for a life of purposeful sin nature is replaced with His righteousness nature. Will we mess up? Absolutely, but it won't be on purpose, and that is where His amazing grace covers us.

We are to love each other, encourage each other in our individual giftings, and be good stewards of His grace, not abusing it to live a life of habitual sin behavior in the name of "freedom in Christ" (boundaries are there for a reason). We are to serve one another without grumbling and complaining (those who would preach). Friends, none of this can be done if we aren't truly walking in the love, holiness, and glory of God. How are we going to reach a lost world when most of the church acts just like them?

My heart is to lead and disciple people into the Kingdom culture of God! I desire so deeply to lead people as Jesus led them, and, honestly, this should be the desire of anyone who serves God. It's part of our mandate to GO and make disciples of all nations—but first, we have to get a new revelation of His holiness and gain a new perspective of the reverential fear of God. Let God have His way IN YOU. There is nothing like it on this earth! In order to walk in God's glory and live a holy lifestyle, we have to be different. We should rejoice in that because we know that we will walk in His glory. How do we live in the very shadows of God's glory just like Peter did? We should

- Have a pure heart;
- Live a Holy lifestyle; and

- Love all.

Father, I ask that You pour Your love into each person praying this prayer. Let them experience You like they never have before. Father, I call down a fresh outpouring of wisdom, revelation, and knowledge onto their lives today. Surround them with Your favor, Your glory, and Your holiness. Give them a fresh boldness to face fear as fearlessly as Joshua did. Let us all be as You on this earth! In Jesus' name, Amen.

Personal Notes:

Day 5: ⟶ Like Precious Faith!

I have decided to skip past 1 Peter 5 because it is written to the Elders/Overseers of the body of Christ. Although as an elder in the church I have studied it out extensively, I believe this is a teaching for "in" the church, not really for devo's. Therefore, we will go straight into 2 Peter. I am only going to cover verses 1-4 in 2 Peter 1, as there is a lot of depth to this and we do not want to skip over any of it. Through this study, I have discovered that Apostle Peter was just amazing. He was able to overcome so much to become a powerful, atmosphere shifting, glory carrier for the Kingdom of God. Oh, do I ever want to be like him!

Over the last year, a lot of my teaching has shifted to Kingdom. The reason for this is because this is our WHY. This is why the body of Christ is on this earth. We are here to bring the culture of the Kingdom to the earth—that's it, point blank. This, of course, will be done in so many different ways, as everyone is gifted and created differently to carry out God's purpose. That's one of the coolest things I think God could do. Think about it: He created each of us with our own little piece to the Kingdom puzzle. I like to think of this as my WHAT – I know WHY I am here, but WHAT is my personal part? Why would He create us with our own little piece? So that we learn that it takes teamwork—we NEED each other because no one person was placed here to do things alone. We are referred to as THE BODY OF CHRIST, not the lone rangers.

This Kingdom business would be so much easier if we could grasp the knowledge of our personal puzzle piece, our what, then team it up with those with whom God connects us. In order for us to carry out God's purpose on this earth, we need to understand that God has given us all that we need to do so. This is what I believe Peter is trying to tell us here in today's study. It is a walk of faith. This letter is written to those who have obtained "like precious" faith by the righteousness of our Father and Jesus Christ.

What on earth is "like precious" faith? When you look that up in the Greek, it actually means of equal value or equal honor. The ESV version says it like this: "To those who have obtained a faith of equal standing with ours." The Apostles carried a level of faith that I don't believe many of us have even barely tapped into. I'm not talking of faith for money, faith for new things, faith for what many of the people of this world and church believe they have faith for. I'm talking about a faith that ushers in the glory of God to a level that none have seen—a faith that believes without a single ounce of doubt that God is going to heal the person in the wheelchair who can't walk, that the cancer in a person's body can literally disappear in the presence of His glory, a faith so strong that we KNOW the divine power and influence we carry. That kind of faith.

Peter goes on to say, "Grace and peace be multiplied [lavished] to you IN the rich knowledge ['the knowing', discernment, to know WELL] of God and of Jesus Christ, as HIS DIVINE POWER has given to us ALL THINGS that pertain to life and godliness, THROUGH the knowledge of Him who called us by glory and virtue." Are you seeing what Peter is saying? I want to go back to walking in the holiness of God for a minute. To walk in the true holiness of God, we have to know the truth of who He is, and we must grasp hold of the knowledge of who Jesus Christ is IN US. It is only IN and THROUGH the knowledge of Him that we are able to receive DIVINE POWER, GRACE and PEACE. This takes "like precious" faith.

Why do we need His divine power working in our lives? Look at the verse again: "His divine power has given us ALL THINGS that pertain to life [zoe- vitality, to live to the fullest] and godliness [holiness, piety]." It is through His divine power that we are able to live the life He has given us to its fullest, and it is through His divine power that we learn to walk in holiness. This is the power Peter and the other Apostles walked in—the power much of the church is missing. This is the power that directs us to our personal puzzle piece, our WHAT – our calling, in the Kingdom mandate. This is the power promised to those who KNOW Him. I want to know Him more and more!

Each one of us is called by glory and virtue. Did you know that? Peter says, "He called us by glory [honor, pleasure] and virtue [excellence], by which have been given to us exceedingly, great and precious promises, that through these [great and precious promises] you may be partakers of HIS DIVINE NATURE [HIS KINGDOM], and it is in His divine nature that we escape the corruption in the world." His great and precious promises are listed all throughout the Word of God. These promises offer us the glory and virtue of Christ as the basis for our growing participation in His divine nature, our growing participation in His Kingdom, and our maturing into our WHAT.

My gosh, there is so much packed in this little piece of 2 Peter, so much! One of the greatest promises is John 14:23: "If anyone loves Me, he will keep My Word; and My Father will love him, and We will come to him and MAKE OUR HOME WITH (IN) HIM." That promise right there is one of glory and virtue. It is through Him IN US that we are able to know Him and become a new creation in Christ, letting go of the old behaviors (corruption of the world) and becoming more like HIM—Christ-like, His Divine Nature, Holy, Glory Carriers, Divine Power Conduits, Kingdom Power Houses with a WHAT that will not stop. Paul was a great example of this. That man, Saul at the time, had a passion for killing Christians. He was ruthless in his pursuit to prove he was right, all in the name of religion, but he had an encounter with Jesus Christ that changed him forever. He was able to take that same passion for proving his own truth and used it to prove THE Truth. Through the knowledge of Jesus Christ IN HIM, he found his part in the Kingdom puzzle, and he never stopped.

All of this is done through "like precious" faith, faith that is equal to that of the first church.

Father teach us to walk in "like precious" faith. Let the truths of Your word soak deep into the recesses of our soul (our mind, our will, our emotions). We know our spirit man is renewed in you, and the faith is already there because You are IN US, so God, we declare that our souls line up and grasp every ounce of truth. Father, we want to be a people holy before You, a people carrying Your glory and walking so close to you that we stay under your shadow, a people who KNOW You and walk IN and THROUGH that knowledge, becoming more and more like You. We will walk in Your divine nature, divine power, glory, and holiness, and we will be Kingdom warriors with a passion that never stops growing. Reunite us to our first love, You and You alone! In Jesus' name, Amen.

Personal Notes:

Day 6: ⟶ *Make Your Choosing Sure*

Today, we will continue in 2 Peter 1, starting with verse 5. Previously, we ended at verse 4, and we were reminded that WE can become partakers of the divine nature of God through His exceedingly and precious promises. It is in living in His divine nature that we are able to escape the corruption that is in the world—the corruption that is brought about because of the sinful desires of those not living in His divine nature. The world's corruption may be all around us, but because of who He is IN US, we do not have to be partakers in it because we are partakers IN HIM.

In the last devo, we talked about "like precious" faith, and how it is through that faith that we receive His promises and walk in His divine power and nature. But Peter is adding on here: he says now that you have a faith equal to ours--"like precious" faith—you need to grow in your knowledge of Jesus Christ. You need to be effective and fruitful in the Kingdom, and this is how. 2 Peter 1:5-8 says, "For this very reason, giving all diligence [or make every effort] to add to your faith, virtue; to virtue, knowledge; to knowledge, self-control; to self-control, perseverance; to perseverance, godliness; to godliness, brotherly kindness; and to brotherly kindness, LOVE. For these qualities are YOURS and are increasing; they keep you from being ineffective or unfruitful in the knowledge of Jesus Christ." God did not call us into His Kingdom in order to be ineffective and unfruitful. In fact, when Jesus speaks to His disciples in Matthew 7,

He explains to them that they need to be aware of false prophets and those in sheep's clothing. He tells them narrow is the gate and difficult is the way which leads to life, and there are few who find it. He explains to them, "You will know them by their fruits.... Every good tree bears good fruit, but a bad tree bears bad fruit, those who bear bad fruit will be cut down and thrown into the fire.... again... by their fruits you will know them!" He wants us to manifest good fruit.

We have everything IN US to walk in the knowledge of Jesus Christ. He was very straightforward when he said, "These qualities ARE yours and are increasing." So, why do you think we have so many unfruitful and ineffective people in the body of Christ? I believe it's because they have chosen not to cultivate (increase) what's already in them. They are not adding to their faith virtue (moral excellence), knowledge (knowing, perceiving), self-control (temperance), perseverance (constancy, continuance), godliness (reverence, HOLINESS, piety), brotherly kindness, and LOVE (*agape*—God-love, unconditional). It is one thing to have the faith to believe in Jesus Christ as our Lord and Savior, but it is another thing to have "like precious" faith built upon the foundation and character of Jesus Christ in order to be the conduit that He can work through to manifest "His Kingdom come, His will be done on earth as it is in heaven." It's time to decrease in SELF and increase in HIM, just like John says in John 3:30: "He must increase, but I must decrease!" We have a transformation mandate, and it is ONLY through HIM that this is possible.

Peter goes on to tell us in verse 9, "For he who lacks these things is shortsighted [seeing only what is near], even to blindness [mentally smoky], and has forgotten that he was cleansed from his old sins." Oh, Father, we ask for mental clarity so that we can see more clearly YOUR heart's desires; give us vision to see not only the near but that which is far off, and help us to grasp the understanding that our old man has passed away and all things have become new IN YOU so that we can grow in the knowledge of You, increase in Your character, and experience true salvation (wholeness) of our soul (our mind, will, and emotions). It is only through this we can truly walk in Your holiness and manifest Your glory.

Verses 10-11 tell us, "Be even more diligent to make your call and election sure, for if you do these things you will never stumble; for so an entrance will be supplied to you abundantly into the everlasting Kingdom of Jesus Christ." In other words, he is informing us that in order to have access to the Kingdom of Jesus Christ (His character, power, authority, freedom, all that His Kingdom consists of) and to never stumble (fall or be offended), we must walk in all that is needed to be fruitful and effective in the knowledge of Jesus Christ, and we must be diligent to make our call (vocation, calling) and election (our choosing) sure. It is only through Him and the knowledge of Jesus Christ that we will truly know our calling, and when we do, we better make our choosing sure. We are reminded in Matthew 22:14, "Many are called, but few are chosen." We could take that back to the KJV where they actually block in the "are" before chosen because that wasn't originally there. In other words, many are called (we are all created with a call from the beginning of creation), but few have chosen or will choose to say yes and to walk in it. Those who do are the ones God can use and will choose. I'm telling you, make your choosing sure (steadfast, stable, firm and of force)!

I want to encourage you today to make a plan—a plan that will help you be more pro-active in seeking God at a deeper level, a plan to fully submerge yourself IN HIM and the knowledge of Jesus Christ. This kind of plan is not something you have to sit around and pray about; it is His will that ALL know Jesus Christ. Set some goals such as giving Him more of your time daily, reading the Word or listening to it someway, or grasping the understanding that you can spend all day in prayerful communication with Him. He wants to be a part of your everyday life and decision making. We are no longer in a time to play with our relationship with God.

Father, I come before you in complete awe. I ask that you forgive me for the times I've chosen not to allow Your character to be cultivated in and seen through me. I ask that You continue to help me decrease so that You can increase in my life. Father, I keep thinking back to Deuteronomy 10:12 where Israel was reminded of what You require of them and of us—that we have a reverential fear of You, that we are to walk in all Your ways, and that we are to LOVE You and serve You with all of our heart and with all our soul. Father give us a healthy reminder of what it means to walk in reverential fear of You. I think sometimes we get so comfortable with life and our walk that we forget. Father, I know that the fear of the Lord is essential to the pursuit of obedience and holiness, and I choose to walk in both of these. As we increase in virtue, knowledge, self-control, perseverance, godliness, brotherly kindness and love, as we add these to our faith and grow in intimacy with Jesus Christ, help us know our WHAT, our purpose in the Kingdom, our specific puzzle piece. Let us make our choosing sure and be steadfast in it. We give you all the glory, all the honor, and all the praise. In Jesus' name, Amen.

Personal Notes:

Day 7: ⟶ Discernment Is Vital

I love how Peter makes sure readers know that he spent personal time with Jesus. In 2 Peter 1: 16-21, he is making it clear that we must realize that nothing he or the other Apostles wrote was made up, but he himself was there when God declared from heaven, "This is my beloved Son, with whom I am well pleased." Verse 19 tells us, "And we have the prophetic word more fully confirmed, to which you will do well to pay attention as to a lamp shining in a dark place, until the day dawns [the season breaks] and the morning star [affirmation, declaration, light] rises [springs up] in your hearts [soul]." He continues with a reminder that pure, true prophecy is not spoken by the will of man but by the Holy Spirit, and any prophetic word given to us must line up with scripture. A prophetic word is sent forth to bring the knowledge (light) of Jesus Christ into our lives and shine into the dark places (the places where there is a lack of knowledge). One thing we have to understand is that every prophetic word spoken over us that is from God's heart will bring revelation and knowledge in areas where we lack knowing or understanding, and it will edify and build us up. This is how God speaks to His children. Never does He condemn, belittle or make His children feel less than! Yes, there will be times when we aren't hearing God for ourselves, and He will send someone to bring a word of correction, but like I said, if it's from the heart of God, even correction is firm yet loving.

Peter is making sure we know the difference between true prophecy and false prophecy because there are so many people out there who claim to be sent from God, and they are speaking things over people that God did not say. The Word of God tells us that the words we speak can bring life or death (Prov. 18:21). The NLT actually says, "The tongue can bring death or life; those who love to talk will reap the consequences." I'm telling you this: if anyone ever speaks over you in the name of God, and it does NOT line up with scripture or even confirm within your spirit, immediately cancel it out because they have just as much power in their words as a true prophet. Better yet, don't let just anyone speak over you. If you don't know them and their life walk, just let them know you would rather they not speak over you.

2 Peter 2 is a firm warning from Peter about false prophets and teachers as well as destructive doctrines. This is why I believe we are in a time in which discernment and the knowledge of the Word is more vital than ever. One of the things God began to speak to me a few years ago was that we were coming into a season where keen discernment was going to be key in every area. There are teachers out there claiming to be teaching the Word of God, yet they are twisting and turning His words to fit their lifestyles and those they want to please. This, my friend, is destructive.

In verse 1, Peter tells us that these false teachers will secretly bring destructive heresies. When you go back to the root of heresies, it means disunion, to take for themselves. These false teachers are crafty in their speech and actions. They gain followers by bringing disunity to the body of Christ. Do we not see this happening all the time? We have people rising up in churches, getting offended or just refusing to submit to authority, and they go through the church in their crafty little ways, planting false prophetic words or seeds into people's minds; then, they step away to build their own church with half of the body of believers from the church to which they formerly belonged. OH MY GOSH, church: this will not only bring destruction in the body as a whole, but Peter tells us this is the recipe for those false teachers to bring swift destruction upon themselves. We've got to wake up and start discerning the spirit, the heart, and the thought behind the choices we make and the voices we hear.

Peter goes on to tell us some pretty hard-core information. I think this is what I'm learning to love about Peter: he wasn't afraid of the crowd and their thoughts toward him. He simply spoke the truth and that was it. Why? Because we are supposed to be leading people to Christ, gaining maturity in Him, and growing disciples who grow more disciples. This takes a truth that not many want to hear! When we mix that truth with God's grace, it changes lives, unlike ear-tickling messages that help people stay in their mess so that they stay dependent on the pastor for all their needs.

Go back and read 2 Peter 2—you will get the gist of what I'm talking about, but it's too much to add here. I will reiterate here, though, that Peter did say this: "The Lord knows how to deliver the godly out of temptations." This tells me that when we are following God with all that's in us and we mess up—you know, we hear a word and feel like it was all God, so we act on it not realizing that it wasn't Him? He will deliver us from that! He goes on to tell us that those who walk as teachers and prophets in a carnal mindset, brushing things off as if it's not important, those who are desiring the tainted and contaminated words that are being thrown around out there and those who defy authority and those who speak against those God has placed over them—false teachers, false prophets or even prophets gone astray—according to verse 17, they are wells without water and storm clouds that darken but don't produce rain. Like I've said over and over, DISCERNMENT IS KEY in this day and age.

One of the things Peter points out is that these false teachers will promise liberty and freedom, yet they are so enslaved in bondage themselves that they lead new believers back into bondage, and the entangling cycle of bondage just keeps building. In order to walk in the true holiness of our God, we must be watchful of those we allow in our lives. Some people just do not have a place to speak into us. I want to encourage you, as you allow people into your life, check out their fruit. Does their fruit represent the holy character of our Father? Do they walk as Jesus walked? Are they portraying His image in this world? Remember, we are told in Matthew 7:20 that we will know them by their fruit!

    Father, I personally want to repent for allowing people to speak into my life who were not supposed to be speaking. I ask that every unfruitful and false word spoken be uprooted from my life in Jesus' name.

Father, I declare over myself a spirit of discernment that is keen and wise but not judgmental. I declare a spirit of wisdom, revelation, and knowledge to begin to see truth as truth and throw off anything that has been twisted or is deceptive. Father continue to guide me into all truth so that I can be a conduit of YOU to this world, so that I can be the light (knowledge) of Jesus Christ in the dark places (lack of understanding). In Jesus' name, Amen.

Personal Notes:

CONNECT WITH

Sabrina

SABRINALKLASSEN.COM

*Cover Photo by Morgan Glocker Photography
*Hair by Claudette Jonker

Made in the USA
Columbia, SC
23 May 2022